AF575834

Commendations for *The Baptist Vision*

"What a gift it is to see this wonderful work come to life. Emerson and Stamps are good guides, building Baptist doctrine and practice on the foundation of Scripture and tracing it through the course of church history while pointing us to a vision of the future. I hope *The Baptist Vision* finds its way into homes, classrooms, and churches, beginning with my own."

—*Matthew Boswell, pastor, The Trails Church and assistant professor of church music and worship, The Southern Baptist Theological Seminary*

"Matt Emerson and Luke Stamps, two theological voices with expanding influence, have provided a helpful introduction to the distinctive beliefs and practices of Baptists. The authors contend that these distinctives are grounded in Scripture and informed by developments within orthodox, catholic, reformational, and evangelical Christianity. While not all readers will agree with all the conclusions offered in *The Baptist Vision*, those who wish to be involved in discussions about the future of Baptists in general, and Southern Baptists in particular, will find this book to be important reading. This volume will be appreciated by students and church leaders alike."

—*David S. Dockery, president and distinguished professor of theology, Southwestern Baptist Theological Seminary*

"I have wanted someone to write a book like this for years. While there are many helpful works on Baptist identity and distinctives, *The Baptist Vision* is in a class by itself. It is fresh without being faddish, constructive while remaining thoroughly conservative, and pastoral without being pragmatic. Matt Emerson and Luke Stamps are first-rate scholars and committed Baptist churchmen. With this book, they have provided Baptists with a resource that will be assigned in classrooms, read on church staff retreats, and taught through in local churches for many years to come. I give it my highest recommendation and trust the Holy Spirit will use it to the ongoing renewal of Baptist faith and practice."

—*Nathan A. Finn, professor of faith and culture, North Greenville University*

"Some years ago, I wrote an essay calling for the renewal of Baptist theology. This well-crafted volume is evidence that such a renascence is actually taking place. Without compromising historic distinctives, Emerson and Stamps deftly place the Baptist saga in the context of the wider Christian family—where it belongs. A welcome contribution to a conversation that needs to continue."

—*Timothy George, distinguished professor of divinity, Beeson Divinity School of Samford University*

"For those who may be struggling with what it means to be a Baptist in the twenty-first century, this book is for you! Matthew Emerson and Luke Stamps have produced a work that is faithful to Scripture and distinctively Baptist. Highly recommended."

—Keith Harper, senior professor of Baptist studies, Southeastern Baptist Theological Seminary (Retired)

"Emerson and Stamps have written a superb, and highly accessible, study of what it means to be a Baptist. Solidly grounded in both Scripture and Baptist history, it succeeds brilliantly in depicting the nature of this important theological and spiritual tradition."

—Michael A. G. Azad Haykin, professor of church history and biblical spirituality, The Southern Baptist Theological Seminary

"Dr. Herschel H. Hobbs was a resident preacher-theologian. In his preaching he theologized and in his theology he preached. The product of his preaching and theology duo is doxology—an act of worship of the sovereign God. This volume mirrors Dr. Hobbs's doctrinal identity and is valuable for all who want to have practical and culturally relevant theology and practice. It moves readers beyond beliefs we hold to convictions that hold us during the doctrinal vicissitudes of life, and carries us from orthodoxy to orthopraxy."

—Robert Smith Jr., distinguished professor of divinity, Beeson Divinity School of Samford University

"In *The Baptist Vision*, Matthew Emerson and Lucas Stamps provide an even-handed description of and winsome, aspirational vision for Baptist life. They offer to people a resource by which Baptists of distant stripes can remember where we came from and why we hold our distinctive beliefs, and consider who we want to be in this generation and the next. This book should be a go-to resource for orienting Baptists to who we are and who we can be."

—Christy Thornton, director of discipleship content, The Summit Church, Raleigh-Durham, North Carolina

"*The Baptist Vision* is that singularly compelling introduction to church life I wish I had written. Every generation must wrestle with its own identity by engaging with holy Scripture, with their church's tradition, and with the world in which we now live. Emerson and Stamps herein offer the rising generation the key text needed both to enter and to improve upon the ongoing Baptist conversation which seeks to answer critical questions like, Who are we?, and What must we do? May this book have the wide use and deep impact it richly deserves."

—Malcolm B. Yarnell III, research professor of theology, Southwestern Baptist Theological Seminary

Commendations for Hobbs College Library

"This series honors a wonderful servant of Christ with a stellar lineup of contributors. What a gift to the body of Christ! My hope and prayer is that it will be widely read and used for the glory of God and the good of his Church."

—Daniel L. Akin, president, Southeastern Baptist Theological Seminary

"This series is a must-have, go-to resource for everyone who is serious about Bible study, teaching, and preaching. The authors are committed to the authority of the Bible and the vitality of the local church. I am excited about the kingdom impact of this much-needed resource."

—Hance Dilbeck, president and chief executive officer of GuideStone

"This series offers an outstanding opportunity for leaders of all kinds to strengthen their knowledge of God, his word, and the manner in which we should engage the culture around us. Do not miss this opportunity to grow as a disciple of Jesus and as a leader of his church."

—Micah Fries, director of engagement, glocal.net, and the director of programs, Multi-Faith Neighbor's Network

"The best resources are those that develop the church theologically while instructing her practically in the work of the Great Commission. Dr. Thomas has assembled an impressive host of contributors for a new set of resources that will equip leaders at all levels who want to leave a lasting impact for the gospel. Dr. Hobbs exemplified the pastor-leader-theologian, and it's inspiring to see a series put out in his name that so aptly embodies his ministry and calling."

—J.D. Greear, pastor, The Summit Church, Raleigh-Durham, NC, and former president, the Southern Baptist Convention

THE BAPTIST VISION

HOBBS COLLEGE LIBRARY

THE BAPTIST VISION

Faith and Practice

for a Believers' Church

MATTHEW Y. EMERSON

and R. LUCAS STAMPS

The Baptist Vision: Faith and Practice for a Believers' Church

Published by B&H Academic®
Brentwood, Tennessee

ISBN: 978-1-0877-5428-4

Dewey Decimal Classification: 286
Subject Heading: BAPTISTS \ SOUTHERN BAPTISTS \
BAPTISTS--DOCTRINES

The web addresses referenced in this book were live and correct at the time of the book's publication but may be subject to change.

Printed in the United States of America
30 29 28 27 26 25 VP 1 2 3 4 5 6 7 8 9 10

To
Al Jackson and Steven Wade,
faithful shepherds
who instilled within us
the Baptist vision
of Christ
and his church.

Contents

About the Library

The Hobbs College Library equips Christians with tools for growing in the faith and for effective ministry. The library trains its readers in three major areas: Bible, theology, and ministry. The series originates from the Herschel H. Hobbs College of Theology and Ministry at Oklahoma Baptist University, where biblical, orthodox, and practical education lies at its core. Training the next generation was important for the great Baptist statesman Dr. Herschel H. Hobbs, and the Hobbs College that bears his name fosters that same vision.

The Hobbs College Library: Biblical. Orthodox. Practical.

Introduction: The Baptist Vision

Being a Baptist can sometimes feel like a liability. There are Christian traditions that are older.[1] There are Christian traditions that have more members, more resources, more institutions, more influential theologians, and more world leaders. Baptists are sometimes regarded (with more or less warrant) as less intellectually sophisticated, less theologically robust, more sectarian, and more censorious. Baptists have sometimes garnered attention for scandal and abuse, for hatred and division.

Now in its fifth century, the Baptist movement has a membership in the tens of millions worldwide, and that number becomes hundreds of millions if you include all baptistic (that is, non-infant-baptizing) churches. There are Baptists on every inhabited continent. Baptists are numbered among the world's politicians, scholars, and artists. Still, the strength of the Baptist movement, both in its seminal years and today, lies in its resonance with the faith of the common person. Baptist polity is democratic, and, in many ways, so is its spirituality. Baptists have no pope, no priests (other than the "priest at every elbow," as one Baptist put it), and no central ecclesiastical authority other than the lordship of Christ over every conscience and every local assembly of covenanted members.[2] Baptist spirituality is a worldwide phenomenon and retains its vibrancy

[1] This assumes we date the origin of Baptists as we know them to sometime in the early seventeenth century. Of course, Baptists also believe that our doctrines are grounded in the deepest root of the Christian tradition: the apostolic teaching of the New Testament. We will discuss Baptist origins more in Part 1: Foundations.

[2] Carlyle Marney, *Priests to Each Other* (Macon: Smyth and Helwys, 2014), xi.

even in the secular West. Baptists at their best are firmly situated within historic Christian orthodoxy, but their dogged commitment to the supreme authority of Scripture and their quest for more light from the Word has given the movement a nimbleness and vitality that renders it relevant in each successive generation.

Baptists are not often known for their academic theologians, though there are some exceptional theologians in the Baptist tradition. Benjamin Keach, Thomas Grantham, Thomas Monck, John Gill, Andrew Fuller, J. P. Boyce, E. Y. Mullins, Carl F. H. Henry, Millard Erickson, and many more could be mentioned. But Baptists have most often made their imprint elsewhere. The best-selling allegorist John Bunyan; the pioneering missionaries George Liele, William Carey, and Adoniram Judson; the preachers Charles Spurgeon, Adrian Rogers, and John Piper; the social reformers Walter Rauschenbusch, Martin Luther King Jr., and Jerry Falwell (a theologically diverse trio, to be sure); the evangelist Billy Graham—these have been among the more influential figures in Baptist history. But again, the heart of the Baptist movement rests in the pews—the anonymous faithful who teach Sunday School; sing in the choir; volunteer at Vacation Bible School; evangelize their children, neighbors, and coworkers; and support global missions through their tithes and offerings.

Being a Baptist is not just a liability; it is also a tremendous asset. For many of us, it is the community of faith that has given birth to our faith and taught us to love Jesus, read the Bible, and share the gospel. It is the community that has educated, ordained, and commissioned us, sustaining the little ship of our faith in the stormy seas of life and death. Baptists are not perfect. We have our warts. We have stains on our past and present. We have areas of needed growth and development. But we, too, are a part of the people of God, the body and bride of Christ, and the temple of the Holy Spirit.

This book is an introduction to and a celebration of the faith and practice of Baptists. Over the years, we have known Baptists who have felt the need to leave the Baptist tradition for what they perceived as greener denominational pastures. Sometimes it was for theological and confessional reasons. Sometimes it was for liturgical and sacramental reasons. Sometimes it was for personal and psychological reasons. To be sure, we begrudge no one's spiritual journey, provided it remains oriented toward the Lord Jesus Christ as he is revealed in Holy Scripture. But we have often lamented that many leave without really wrestling with the biblical, theological, and spiritual strengths of the Baptist vision. Many are insufficiently catechized in the Baptist faith, history, biblical theological rationale, and practical and spiritual appeal. This introduction to Baptist beliefs and practices aims to provide a partial remedy to this need. Its intended audience is twofold: Baptists themselves, and those who may be curious about us. It has, thus, both a formative and an apologetic (and even ecumenical) aim. It is our hope that this introduction would present a biblical, charitable, and winsome presentation of the Baptist vision.

We have titled this work *The Baptist Vision*. As such, the book aims to be primarily descriptive, but, in a measured sense, it intends to be prescriptive as well. On the one hand, our aim is to explore the ways that Baptists have historically viewed the Christian faith, Holy Scriptures, identity and mission of the church, and life of Christian discipleship. But we will also suggest a particular vision for the Baptist future, one that is more explicitly and intentionally positioned as a renewal movement within the one, holy, catholic, and apostolic church. As we will argue in the first part of this book, Baptists are Christians first, and a particular expression of Protestant and evangelical Christianity at that. Only from this "little-c" catholic and reformational position can Baptists effectively make their case for continued reformation and renewal according to the Scriptures.

Closely related to this theme of vision is the theme of pilgrimage. We set our sights on Christ and his present and future kingdom as we make our way toward our heavenly home. In his famous allegory, *The Pilgrim's Progress*, the Baptist preacher John Bunyan movingly describes every Christian's journey as a pilgrim, a wayfarer, on the road to the Celestial City. This description is especially fitting for Baptist Christians, given our distinctive emphasis on the church as a pilgrim people: a people called out of and set apart from the world by a grace-enabled and willing faith, and sealed in believers' baptism. As pilgrims, Baptists recognize that no theological system is perfect this side of glory. And so, we seek more light from the Word, as we reform even longstanding beliefs and practices according to Scripture.

The book is divided into three parts. In the first part, we explore the theological foundations of the Baptist movement. Here, we situate the Baptist faith in its "little-c" catholic context (that is, the orthodox theology of the historic, universal church), its Protestant or reformational context, and its evangelical context. We also survey the covenant theology that undergirds the Baptist understanding of the church in God's redemptive plan. In the second part, we exposit the major Baptist distinctives, the matrix of beliefs that mark out the Baptist vision as a distinct theological and ecclesiastical movement: a believers' church, believers' baptism, covenantal Communion, congregationalism, and religious liberty. In the final part, we examine some important Baptist practices that emerge from these Baptist beliefs: corporate worship, a life of holiness, and the urgency of missions and evangelism.

We write as two Southern Baptists, and our perspectives are shaped by this context. Baptists in other denominational or national contexts would undoubtedly write a somewhat different account. We have drawn on some of these accounts ourselves, but our primary ecclesial context will be apparent to the reader. Furthermore, we write as "capital-B" Baptists. It has become fashionable to broaden the vision of what it means to be Baptist by opting for the lowercase designation, "baptist," as a way of bringing in the Anabaptist and broader believers' church traditions. While we hope that Christians from these wider circles will benefit from reading our account, we maintain that a focus on the Baptist tradition proper can serve as a kind of "home base," welcoming both agreement and dissent among the various baptistic communions.

A focus on Baptist beliefs and practices can serve not only our own people and churches but also the broader body of Christ. We echo the conviction of Baptist theologian and historian Timothy George that a focus on the particularity of the Baptist vision can serve the unity of the universal church and its mission to testify to the lordship of Christ:

> Particularity in the service of unity? Yes, by all means, let us maintain, undergird, and strengthen our precious Baptist distinctives: our commitment to a regenerate church membership, believers' baptism by immersion in the name of the triune God, our stand for unfettered religious liberty, and all the rest but let us do this not so that people will say how great the Baptists are but rather what a great Savior the Baptists have, what a great God they serve. May they be able to say, "Just look at those Baptist Christians, see how they love one another. See how they work together with other believers. See how they put others

> ahead of themselves. You know, I think I'll give a listen to what they are saying about all of this Jesus Christ suff."[3]

---

[3] Timothy George, "Is Jesus a Baptist?" *First Things*, August 12, 2013, accessed October 10, 2023, https://www.firstthings.com/web-exclusives/2013/08/is-jesus-a-baptist.

PART I

FOUNDATIONS

CHAPTER 1

Catholic: Baptists and Christian Orthodoxy

As we consider the theological identity of Baptists, we begin from the foundations: historic Christian orthodoxy, or catholicity. These terms need to be properly defined from the outset in order to avoid confusion. *Orthodoxy* simply means right teaching, as opposed to heresy or heterodoxy, false teaching. To speak of Baptists as orthodox, we do not mean to identify with "capital-O" Orthodoxy, the branch of Christianity prominent in the Mediterranean world, eastern Europe, and Russia. Instead, we simply mean to communicate that Baptists are Christians in recognizably historic terms. Similarly, *catholicity* simply connotes the Baptists' place in the universal church. The word *catholic* literally means "in respect to the whole." While the New Testament most often speaks of the church (*ekklēsia*) in local terms, it also makes reference to the church in this collective, universal sense (e.g., Eph 1:22; 3:21; 5:22–33). To confess the church's catholicity, then, is to embrace its universal scope and its worldwide dimension—the body of Christ that transcends space and time, province and denomination. To speak of Baptists as catholic, we do not intend to say that Baptists should wish to be "capital-C" Catholic, or Roman Catholic. As we will see in chapter two, Baptists, as Protestants, dissent from Roman Catholicism in some decisive ways. But we do share in common with all who claim the Christian religion certain foundational doctrines, which constitute the Baptist tradition as a renewal movement from within what the Nicene Creed calls the "one, holy, catholic, and apostolic church."[1] In this chapter, we will highlight the catholic commitments of the Baptist vision with regard to two cardinal doctrines: Trinity and Christology. As we will see, Baptists, from their origins in seventeenth-century English Separatism, have taken great pains to demonstrate their conformity to the faith of the whole church on these foundational doctrines, which were revealed in the Scriptures, and which were given creedal expression by the early church fathers.[2]

The Blessed Trinity

The first hymn in the *Baptist Hymnal*, "Holy, Holy, Holy," frames Baptist worship in explicitly trinitarian terms: "Holy, holy, holy! Merciful and mighty! God in three persons, blessed Trinity!"[3] Baptists confess, along with all Christians, that God is one in being or essence and three in persons. We will consider the doctrine of the Trinity from three vantage points: God's life in himself, God's work of creation, and God's work of redemption. We will then demonstrate that this catholic doctrine has been the confession of Baptists from their origins.

The Christian life begins and ends in God. He is the infinitely Blessed One. As the *Baptist Catechism* puts it, "God is a Spirit,

---

[1] "The Nicene Creed," accessed June 18, 2024, https://www.bcponline.org/General/nicene_creed.html.

[2] For a recent assessment of catholicity from a free church perspective (which includes Baptist churches), see C. Ryan Fields, *Local and Universal: A Free Church Account of Ecclesial Catholicity*, Studies in Christian Doctrine and Scripture (Downers Grove: IVP Academic, 2024).

[3] "Holy, Holy, Holy," in *The Baptist Hymnal* (Nashville: Convention, 1991), 2.

infinite, eternal, and unchangeable in his being, wisdom, power, holiness, justice, goodness, and truth."[4] All perfections are found in him as the fount of all goodness, truth, and beauty. Even if nothing else existed, even if he had never chosen to create the universe, God would still exist in perfect beatitude and love as Father, Son, and Holy Spirit. God is one in essence and three in persons. There is only one God, a truth affirmed in both the Old Testament and the New Testament. And yet, this one God exists eternally as three distinct persons, who differ from one another not by essence but by relation, as the influential Nicene Creed (AD 325/381) summarizes. The three persons are one in essence. They share all the same essential attributes (omniscience, omnipotence, holiness, goodness, and so on). Indeed, they share a numerically singular essence or nature. They only differ according to what has come to be known as the eternal relations of origin. The Father has his origin from no one, but he is the eternal origin of the Son and Spirit. The Father is not the creator of the Son and Spirit, since the three are coequal and co-eternal; they are the very same God.[5] But the Son and Spirit eternally come forth from the Father. These relations of origin are utterly unique in that they are both eternal and internal to the life of God: they never had a beginning, do not produce a second and third being, and are distinct modes of existence within the very same being of God. The Son is eternally "begotten" of the Father (John 1:14, 18 ASV), and the Holy Spirit eternally "proceeds" from the Father and Son (John 15:26). These relations are difficult to understand, but they are implied in the very names that God uses to identify himself.

---

[4] "The Baptist Catechism," in *The Baptist Confession and the Baptist Catechism* (Birgmingham: Solid Ground, 2010), 94.

[5] The notion that the Father created the Son is especially associated with the ancient heresy of Arianism. For a collection of primary sources on these issues, see William G. Rusch, ed., *The Trinitarian Controversy*, Sources of Early Christian Thought (Minneapolis: Fortress, 1980).

The words *Father* and *Son* connote this notion of origin. Fathers generate sons; sons come from fathers. Even the name *Spirit* tells us something about the identity of the third person. He is, as many medieval theologians liked to say, "spirated," or breathed out, by the Father and Son. He is the shared Spirit of both the Father and the Son and closely identified in Scripture with the themes of love and gifts.[6]

The created universe is the handiwork of this eternally Blessed One. Everything comes from God and, in its own way, leads back to him. He is the source, cause, end, and goal of all that exists. God created the world, as he does with all of his external acts, precisely as Father, Son, and Holy Spirit. The Father is, as the Nicene Creed puts it, the "maker of all things visible and invisible," who created the world through his eternal Word and Spirit.[7] The Son is the Logos, the Word of God, from whom and for whom all things exist (John 1:1–3; Col 1:16). The Spirit, too, is the agent of creation, the One who "hovered" over the face of the waters, bringing all created reality to its completion and perfection (Gen 1:2). Moreover, God is also the providential Lord of all creation, sustaining the world in existence by his will and governing the world and all of its affairs according to his eternal decree. And God does all of this, not as a solitary person, nor as three distinct beings working in harmony, but as a single being who works inseparably as Father, Son, and Holy Spirit.

These personal relations are also revealed by God's activity in salvation history. Because the Son is eternally from the Father, it is fitting that he is the One sent by the Father to redeem the world.

---

[6] For a helpful treatment of historic trinitarian theology, see Fred Sanders, *The Triune God*, New Studies in Dogmatics (Grand Rapids: Zondervan, 2016).

[7] "The Nicene Creed," accessed June 18, 2024, https://www.bcponline.org/General/nicene_creed.html.

Because the Holy Spirit eternally proceeds from the Father and Son, it is fitting that he is the One sent by the Father and Spirit to indwell and empower believers. The works of God reveal who God really is and what he is really like. In more technical theological language, the temporal "missions" (the sendings of the Son and Spirit in time) externalize and reveal the eternal "processions" (the relations of origin). Just as with creation, so also with redemption God's work is unified and inseparable. Even though only the Son takes on human flesh and dies as a ransom for sin, it is the triune God who accomplishes salvation. In love, the Father sends the Son for the redemption of the world. In obedience, the Son accomplishes salvation through his work as the mediator. In grace, the Spirit applies this work of redemption to believers through regeneration and sanctification. In each of these works, it is the one triune God who saves his people from sin and death.[8]

God is triune (one-in-three) in his eternal being, works of creation and providence, and gracious work of redemption. This historic Christian teaching is foundational to the Baptist vision. From their origins in the seventeenth century, Baptists have been eager to demonstrate that they are saying nothing new regarding this cardinal Christian doctrine, echoing the terms of the early Christian councils, such as Nicaea (325) and Constantinople (381). Though the last two centuries have seen the rise of more "liberal" Baptists who call into question certain aspects of Christian orthodoxy, the Baptist confessional tradition has been noticeably orthodox. The early Baptist confessions of faith in particular deliberately used the language of the traditional doctrine of the Trinity. For example, consider the Second London Baptist Confession, the most influential confession of

[8] For more on unity and distinctions in the triune God's activities, see Matthew Y. Emerson and Brandon D. Smith, *Beholding the Triune God: The Inseparable Work of Father, Son, and Holy Spirit* (Wheaton: Crossway, 2024).

faith in Baptist history. The statement was adopted by the Particular Baptist assembly in 1677 and published in 1689. It was deliberately patterned after the Westminster Confession of Faith, a Presbyterian confession drafted by the Westminster Assembly in 1646. The same document was adapted by the Congregationalists in their Savoy Declaration of 1658. By echoing these other confessions of faith, the Baptists wished to demonstrate their solidarity with their fellow Protestants and the rich heritage of trinitarian reflection inherited from the patristic era, that is, the era of the church fathers. The Second London Confession is markedly orthodox in its statement on the Trinity:

> In this divine and infinite Being there are three subsistences, the Father, the Word or Son, and Holy Spirit, of one substance, power, and eternity, each having the whole divine essence, yet the essence undivided: the Father is of none, neither begotten nor proceeding; the Son is eternally begotten of the Father; the Holy Spirit proceeding from the Father and the Son; all infinite, without beginning, therefore but one God, who is not to be divided in nature and being, but distinguished by several peculiar relative properties and personal relations; which doctrine of the Trinity is the foundation of all our communion with God, and comfortable dependence on Him.[9]

The main contours of the doctrine of the Trinity are all present in this statement. The three divine persons are one in essence. Each has the whole divine essence. In other words, each divine person is truly and fully God. The persons are distinct "subsistences," distinct

---

[9] "Second London Baptist Confession of Faith," in *Baptist Confessions of Faith*, eds., William L. Lumpkin and Bill J. Leonard, Article 2.3.

modes of existence in the one divine essence.[10] They differ only according to their relations of origin: the Father is unbegotten, the Son is eternally begotten from the Father, and the Spirit eternally proceeds (or comes forth) from the Father and Son. These "relative properties and personal relations" mark the three persons as really distinct, but they do not divide the shared essence of the Godhead. This doctrine is the foundation of our communion with God and our "comfortable" dependence on God, a dependence that brings us saving comfort and peace.

Other Baptist confessions and early Baptist writings likewise teach this classic doctrine. The General Baptist Orthodox Creed uses the same language as the Second London Confession: one essence, three subsistences, and distinguished by eternal relations of origin. It connects the doctrine to the key Baptist distinctive: the baptism of believers in the name of the Father, Son, and Holy Spirit (Matt 28:18–20).[11] Baptist theologians such as the seventeenth-century General Baptist Thomas Monck and the eighteenth-century Particular Baptist John Gill wrote influential treatises on the doctrine of the Trinity. The *Baptist Faith and Message* (1925, revised in 1963 and 2000), while using more modern language, nonetheless affirms the same basic teaching: "The eternal triune God reveals Himself to us as Father, Son, and Holy Spirit, with distinct personal attributes, but without division of nature, essence, or being."[12] The confession

[10] But note well, the persons are distinct modes of "being," not merely distinct modes of "revelation," as in the ancient heresy of Sabellianism, or modalism. For a discussion of the modalist heresy, see Thomas Joseph White, OP, *The Trinity: On the Nature and Mystery of the One God*, Thomistic Ressourcement Series (Washington, DC: Catholic University of America Press, 2022), 120–22.

[11] "The Orthodox Creed," Article 3, in *Baptist Confessions of Faith,* eds. Lumpkin and Leonard, 301–302.

[12] *The Baptist Faith and Message* 2000, Article 1, Southern Baptist Convention, accessed June 24, 2024, https://bfm.sbc.net/bfm2000/#ii.

makes it clear that these persons are not simply modes of God's manifestation to us but are eternal and fully divine persons. In sum, the Baptist vision is founded upon the one true God, the blessed Trinity, who exists eternally in three distinct persons: Father, Son, and Holy Spirit.

The Story of Jesus

Another beloved hymn from the *Baptist Hymnal* picks up our second foundational catholic doctrine: "Tell me the story of Jesus, Write on my heart every word; Tell me the story most precious, Sweetest that ever was heard."[13] The hymn recounts the incarnation and birth, fasting, temptations, suffering, death, and resurrection of Jesus Christ for the salvation of the world. The doctrine of "Christology" summarizes this teaching under two heads: the person and the work of Jesus Christ, or his identity and mission.

Who is Jesus?

No question is more pressing for humanity, more decisive for our flourishing in this life and for our salvation in the next, and more important for understanding what it means to be a Baptist: "But you, who do you say that I am?" (Luke 9:20). There have been many answers to this question both in the ancient world and today. Some consider Jesus to be a prophet, a preacher of timeless morals, or even the Messiah of Israel. Each of these answers captures a portion of the truth, but they stop short of the fullest answer we can give biblically. In brief, the New Testament teaches that Jesus is the eternal Word of the Father, who in the fullness of time "became flesh," and took a true human nature to himself, without ceasing to be God,

---

[13] "Tell Me the Story of Jesus," in *The Baptist Hymnal*, 122.

so that he might fulfill God's promises of salvation both for Israel and the whole world. In the New Testament, Jesus is presented as one who is truly divine: he has the attributes of God, performs the works of God, bears the names of God, and receives the worship of God. And yet, this same person is also truly human (Heb 2:17): He is born, grows and develops, hungers, thirsts, grows weary, weeps, is moved to righteous anger, suffers, dies, and is raised in a glorious resurrection body, in which he will return on the last day to judge the living and the dead.

In order to explain this rich biblical teaching, the early church fathers came to speak about Jesus as a single person with two distinct natures.[14] Indeed, he is the eternal second person of the Trinity, who became truly human without ceasing to be truly God. The early centuries witnessed many heretical teachings about Jesus. Some took him to be merely human (the Ebionites). Some believed he was the first and greatest of God's creatures (the Arians). Some maintained positions that made him only partly human (the Docetists, the Apollinarians, and the Eutychians). Some effectively split him into two persons, the Son of God and the Son of Mary (the Nestorians). Each of these ancient heresies sacrifices at least one part of the biblical teaching in order to account for the others. The classic definition of the person of Christ, articulated at the Council of Chalcedon in 451, seeks to account for all that the Scriptures say of the Lord: Christ is one person (Greek, *hypostasis*) with two natures—the nature of God that he shares eternally with the Father and Spirit, and a distinct human nature (body and soul) which he assumed in the incarnation.

---

[14] The definition of the Council of Chalcedon (451) marks the high-water mark for the two-natures Christology. For a collection of primary sources on the early Christological developments, including the texts of the ecumenical councils, see Edward R. Hardy, ed., *Christology of the Later Fathers* (Louisville: Westminster John Knox, 1954).

These two natures are united in the person of the Son (hence the doctrine of the "hypostatic union"), and yet they retain their distinct properties. As the church fathers often put it, without ceasing to be what he was (God the Son), he became what he previously was not (truly human). He did not surrender any of his divine attributes in order to become incarnate; rather, he remained "in the form of God," even as he veiled his majesty by taking "the form of a servant" so that he might suffer, die, and be raised for our salvation (Phil 2:6–7). He had to be "made like his brothers in every respect," taking a true human nature (body and soul), "so that he might become a merciful and faithful high priest in the service of God" (Heb 2:17 ESV).[15]

Just as the early Baptists followed the Nicene understanding of the Trinity, they explicitly affirm the language of the Chalcedonian understanding of the person of Christ. For example, the Baptist Catechism (late seventeenth century) echoes the language of the Westminster Shorter Catechism in its questions and answers on the person of Christ:

> Question 24: Who is the Redeemer of God's elect?
> Answer: The only Redeemer of God's elect is the Lord Jesus Christ, who, being the eternal Son of God, became man, and so was and continueth to be God and man in two distinct natures, and one person for ever.
>
> Question 25: How did Christ, being the Son of God become man?

[15] For a summary of patristic Christology and its reception in early Baptist theology, see R. Lucas Stamps, "Baptists, Classic Christology, and the Christian Tradition," in *Baptists and the Christian Tradition: Towards an Evangelical Baptist Catholicity*, ed. Matthew Y. Emerson, Christopher W. Morgan, and R. Lucas Stamps (Nashville: B&H Academic, 2020), 81–107.

> Answer: Christ the Son of God became man by taking to himself a true body, and a reasonable soul; being conceived by the power of the Holy Spirit in the womb of the Virgin Mary, and born of her, yet without sin.[16]

Several important aspects of the orthodox doctrine of Christ emerge in these concise answers. First, the person of Christ that we meet in Jesus of Nazareth is the eternal Son of God, the Second Person of the Holy Trinity. There are not two persons involved here (contrary to the ancient Nestorian heresy). The Son of Mary is none other than the eternally begotten Son of God. Second, this one person has two distinct natures: the nature of God and the nature of humanity. He is true God (contrary to Arianism) and true man (contrary to Docetism). Furthermore, this personal union is not a temporary state. The Son of God remains incarnate even now in the heavenly sanctuary, and he will return in his risen humanity to judge the living and the dead and to consummate his eternal kingdom. Third, the human nature he assumed in the incarnation is complete: body and soul (contrary to Apollinarianism). In becoming human, Christ partook of Mary's humanity and thus can serve as the Savior of humanity, as the Son of David and the Last Adam. This is a rich statement of historic, catholic Christology. The same picture emerges in other Baptist confessional symbols, as well as in important Baptist theological works.[17]

What Did Jesus Do for Our Salvation?

At the heart of what it means to be a Baptist is a personal faith response to the gospel of Jesus Christ. The word *gospel*, of course,

---

16 "The Baptist Catechism," Questions 24 and 25, 98.

17 See the "Second London Baptist Confession of Faith," Article 7, in *Baptist Confessions*, ed., William L. Lumpkin and Bill J. Leonard, 246–47. The Orthodox

means good news (Greek, *euangelion*). The content of the gospel is the person and work of Jesus Christ. As Paul instructs us, the gospel concerns God's Son, who was "descended from David according to the flesh and was declared to be the Son of God in power according to the Spirit of holiness by his resurrection from the dead, Jesus Christ our Lord" (Rom 1:3–4 ESV). The good news of the saving kingdom is quite simply Jesus himself, in his humanity and deity and in his work of redemption through his death and resurrection. Elsewhere, Paul summarizes his gospel in an almost creedal form:

> For I delivered to you as of first importance what I also received: that Christ died for our sins in accordance with the Scriptures, that he was buried, that he was raised on the third day in accordance with the Scriptures, and that he appeared to Cephas, then to the twelve (1 Cor 15:3–5 ESV).

So, the gospel is the person of Christ, not considered in the abstract, but considered with reference to his saving work. He died for our sins. He was buried. He was raised. He appeared. "Gospel" language proliferates among Christians. We seek to be gospel-driven, gospel-centered, and gospel-saturated. These are wonderful aspirations, but if we are not careful, the glory of the gospel can be lost by casual usage of the term. We also rush to define all our theological debates as "gospel issues." But the gospel has a very specific content. The gospel influences everything, but not everything is the gospel. The gospel is a particular message: the announcement of God's saving reign and rule through the person and work of Jesus Christ. It

---

Creed is even more detailed in giving the main contours of the historic doctrine of Christ (see "The Orthodox Creed," in *Baptist Confessions*, articles 4–7, pp. 302–305). See also Thomas Monck, *A Cure for the Cankering Error of the New Eutychians* (London, 1673); John Gill, *A Complete Body of Doctrinal and Practical Divinity,* 2 vols. (Grand Rapids: Baker, 1978).

was first heralded by the Lord himself (Mark 1:15), and then embodied by him in his sacrificial death and victorious resurrection and proclaimed by the apostles as the "power of God for salvation to everyone who believes" (Rom 1:16).

We also need to view the gospel in its wide-angle biblical lens. The gospel is centered on the atoning death and resurrection of Christ, but it also entails what John Calvin called "the whole course" of Christ's obedience.[18] It includes his so-called passive obedience of suffering and death, and his active obedience of fulfilling all righteousness.[19] The atonement, the reconciling work of Christ, is multifaceted. It includes all the following:

- His incarnation, through which he takes true humanity into personal union with himself
- His nativity, or birth, from the Virgin's womb
- His life of sinless, law-keeping obedience
- His baptism, in which he identifies with repentant sinners, though he had no need of repentance
- His teachings, his miracles, and his exorcisms
- His transfiguration, which reveals his heavenly glory
- His vicarious, or representative, suffering
- His justice-satisfying, corruption-healing, Satan-destroying, friendship-restoring death on the cross
- His burial and descent to the place of the dead
- His triumphant resurrection from the dead
- His appearances to the apostles
- His ascension to heaven
- His session (seating) at the Father's right hand

---

[18] John Calvin, *Institutes of the Christian Religion*, ed. John T. McNeill, trans. Ford Lewis Battles (Louisville: Westminster John Knox, 1960), 2.16.5.

[19] See Robert A. Peterson, *Salvation Accomplished by the Son: The Work of Christ* (Wheaton: Crossway, 2011).

- His pouring out of the promised Holy Spirit
- His ongoing intercession in the heavenly sanctuary as our great High Priest
- His imminent, personal return to judge the living and the dead and to consummate his everlasting kingdom

How rich is the work of Christ and how glorious the gospel! We encourage you to take a moment to read back through this list of Christ's great works and to give thanks to him for his mercy.

The great ecumenical creeds of the ancient church sought to capture a glimpse of this rich story. Consider, for example, the second article of the Apostles' Creed:

> And [I believe] in Jesus Christ, his only Son, our Lord,
> who was conceived by the Holy Spirit,
> born of the Virgin Mary,
> suffered under Pontius Pilate,
> was crucified, died and was buried;
> he descended to the dead;
> on the third day he rose again from the dead;
> he ascended into heaven,
> and is seated at the right hand of God the Father almighty;
> from there he will come to judge the living and the dead.[20]

Or consider the second article of the Nicene Creed:

> And [I believe] in one Lord Jesus Christ, the only-begotten Son of God, begotten of the Father before all worlds; God of God, Light of Light, very God of very

[20] "The Apostles' Creed," accessed June 18, 2024, https://www.anglicancommunion.org/media/109023/Apostles-Creed.pdf.

> God; begotten, not made, being of one substance with the Father, by whom all things were made. Who, for us men for our salvation, came down from heaven, and was incarnate by the Holy Spirit of the virgin Mary, and was made man; and was crucified also for us under Pontius Pilate; He suffered and was buried; and the third day He rose again, according to the Scriptures; and ascended into heaven, and sits on the right hand of the Father; and He shall come again, with glory, to judge the living and the dead; whose kingdom shall have no end.[21]

Note that these ancient symbols of the Christian faith draw a close connection between the person and the work of Christ. Jesus is who he is so that he can do what he does. And he does what he does only because he is who he is. Only the eternally begotten and incarnate Son of God can save the world. Only the God-man can be the mediator between God and man, and what he does to accomplish our redemption is multifaceted. He did not merely die for our sins. He was conceived and born for us. He was raised for us. He descended and ascended for us. He is returning for us.

This rich depiction of Christ's work is echoed in the Baptist confessional tradition as well. The First London Baptist Confession of Faith (1644) frames Christ's obedience in terms of his threefold office (*munus triplex*): "Touching His office, Jesus Christ only is made the mediator of the new covenant, even the everlasting covenant of grace between God and man, to be perfectly and fully the Prophet, Priest and King of the Church of God for evermore."[22] As Prophet, he "perfectly revealed the whole will of God out of

---

[21] "The Nicene Creed," accessed June 18, 2024, https://www.bcponline.org/General/nicene_creed.html.

[22] "The Orthodox Creed," Article 9, *Baptist Confessions of Faith,* 146–47.

the bosom of the Father, that is needful for His servants to know, believe, and obey." As Priest, Christ "has appeared once to put away sin by the offering and sacrifice of Himself" and "ever lives and sits at the right hand of Majesty, appearing before the face of His Father to make intercession for such as come to the Throne of Grace by that new and living way." And as King, he spiritually governs his church, rules over his enemies, subdues and takes away our sins, and strengthens us in our conflicts with sin and Satan. Other Baptist symbols make the very same points. Baptist authors, preachers, evangelists, and missionaries have been second to none in proclaiming the manifold wisdom of God in the person and work of Jesus Christ.[23]

Conclusion

Before we get to what makes Baptists distinct (part 2 of this book), we need to make clear what makes Baptists Christians. In this chapter, we have described Baptists as catholic in this important and specific sense: Baptists have been eager to affirm historic Christian orthodoxy, especially as it touches on God himself (the Holy Trinity), the person of Christ (the incarnation), and the work of Christ (the atonement). The basic contours of Christian orthodoxy can be seen in the Baptist confessional tradition and in prominent Baptist authors. In short, we are Baptists best when we are Christians first. We can celebrate all that we have in common with fellow believers in other traditions without surrendering what makes us distinctive. And what we share in common with all Christians is a humble, childlike faith in the heart of the biblical message: that "God so loved the

---

[23] The Second London Confession, Articles 10–20, treat Christ's threefold office. See "Second London Baptist Confession of Faith," in *Baptist Confessions*, 159–62.

world, that he gave his only begotten Son, that whosoever believeth on him should not perish, but have eternal life" (John 3:16 ASV).

CHAPTER 2

Reformational: Baptists and the Protestant Reformation

Introduction

Baptists are not only catholic; they are also Protestant, or reformational. The Baptist vision represents a renewal movement from within Protestant Christianity. With their fellow Protestants, Baptists affirm the soteriological and ecclesiological convictions associated with the sixteenth-century Reformation. Baptists agree with both the formal principle of the Reformation (the supreme authority of Scripture alone) and the material principle of the Reformation (justification by faith alone, apart from works). Baptists likewise reject the distinctive claims of the Roman Catholic Church: its claim to be the only true church; its sacramental system; and its understanding of tradition, faith and works, grace and merit, Mary, purgatory, and more.

We speak of Baptists as "reformational," rather than narrowly "Reformed."[1] Baptists have always been divided on questions related

[1] "Reformational" has also been used by Albert Wolters to capture a particular conviction, rooted in the thought of Dutch theologian and politician Abraham Kuyper, that the whole of the created order is to be redeemed through the work of Christ. While we sympathize with some of Kuyper's vision, we are not using the term

to predestination and free will. Some have been more Arminian and some have been more Calvinist in their soteriological convictions. A strength of the Baptist movement is that it has encompassed both of these perspectives and has often brought them into common fellowship and even theological synthesis. The Baptist vision includes both an emphasis on God's sovereign grace and on man's freedom, responsibility, and duty to believe personally in the gospel of Jesus Christ. Baptists have reconciled these mysteries in distinct ways, but the Baptist movement as a whole cannot surrender either side of the tension. "Reformational" also highlights the key Baptist conviction that we are to be "always reforming" according to the norm of Scripture. We even part ways with our fellow Protestants where we believe them to be insufficiently "Reformed" in their understanding of the church and its ordinances.

In this chapter, we will briefly explore the question of Baptist origins and then summarize Baptists' reformational convictions on the doctrines of Scripture and salvation. Baptists emerged in the context of seventeenth-century English Separatism, which in turn emerged in the context of the English Reformation. Understanding these origins and their doctrinal commitments will help Baptists better understand their theological heritage.

Baptist Origins

While this is primarily a book about Baptist beliefs and practices, three major perspectives on historical Baptist origins are worth

---

in this narrow sense. See Albert M. Wolters, *Creation Regained: Biblical Basics for a Reformational Worldview*, 2nd ed. (Grand Rapids: Eerdmans, 2005).

mentioning.[2] In previous generations, a view known as *Baptist successionism* was especially prominent. According to this view, Baptists are neither Catholic nor Protestant but represent a distinct movement that can be traced, through a succession of sectarian groups, all the way back to the New Testament. This idea was often associated with Landmarkism and was popularized by the tract, *The Trail of Blood*, written by J. M. Carroll. Given its tendentious historical and theological claims, few Baptist scholars today adopt this perspective. Another view, known as the *Anabaptist kinship view*, draws a close connection between the early British Baptists and the continental Anabaptists. Baptists who hold this position tend to see Baptist history and theology in continuity with the believers' church theology of the Radical Reformation. Important to this view is the fact that the early Baptist John Smyth had interactions with and eventually joined a Mennonite congregation in Holland. What needs to be further considered, however (and will be in a later chapter), is that Smyth helped to start (with Thomas Helwys) a Baptist church prior to this interaction, and the church actually parted ways with Smyth after his joining with the Anabaptists. They then returned to England as a self-consciously Baptist church under the leadership of Helwys. The *English Separatist view* of Baptist origins is the most historically credible. The early Baptists emerged from congregations that had separated from the established church in order to form assemblies that were more perfectly conformed to the rule of the New Testament. We often speak of these churches as "congregationalist" because they were seeking to form independent congregations of visible saints. Eventually some in these churches

---

[2] For more on Baptist origins, see Anthony L. Chute, Nathan A. Finn, and Michael A. G. Haykin, *The Baptist Story: From English Sect to Global Movement* (Nashville: B&H Academic, 2015), 11–37.

became convinced that the practice of infant baptism was inconsistent with this pursuit.

As a further complication, the story of Baptist beginnings is not one origin story but two: the emergence of the Arminian *General Baptists* under the leadership of Smyth and Helwys in the 1600s and 1610s, and the emergence of the *Particular Baptists* from more Calvinistic Congregationalists in the 1630s and 40s. These groups received their names from their respective views on the extent of Christ's atoning work: General Baptists believed in a general or universal atonement for all, while Particular Baptists believed in a particular or limited atonement for the elect. In the beginning, these groups did not see themselves as parts of the same "pan-Baptist" movement. Eventually they would both adopt the label "Baptist," and in the centuries that followed, they would experience significant theological and institutional cross-pollination.[3]

So, what is the relationship between the early Baptists and the Protestant Reformation? Given the English Separatist understanding of Baptist origins, Baptists can be seen as a renewal movement within seventeenth-century English Protestantism. The Puritans sought to reform the Church of England according to Scripture and to rid it of its "popish" errors. Eventually some Puritans became convinced that they must separate from the establishment in order to form independent assemblies of visible saints. Among the Congregationalist (as opposed to Presbyterian) Separatists, some became convinced infant baptism was not warranted by the New Testament practice and began to practice believers' baptism. It was the Particular Baptists in the 1630s who submitted to believers' baptism by full immersion (the General Baptists had initially practiced believers'

---

[3] See Matthew C. Bingham, *Orthodox Radicals: Baptist Identity in the English Reformation*, Oxford Studies in Historical Theology (Oxford: Oxford University Press, 2019).

baptism by sprinkling). Both groups of Baptists saw themselves in solidarity with their fellow Protestants on the major emphases of the Reformation, especially as it related to the doctrines of Scripture and salvation.

Protestant Bibliology

The Reformation did not seek an overthrow of the church's creedal foundations on the cardinal doctrines of the Trinity and the incarnation. The Reformers and their heirs in the post-Reformation period were eager to affirm these ancient truths. Thus, to be "reformational" is also to remain fully "catholic." But the Reformation did usher in a series of reforms, especially as it relates to the locus of religious authority (the relationship between Scripture and tradition) and the application of the work of Christ to the believer (the doctrine of salvation), both of which spawned the ecclesiological reforms of the various Protestant denominations.

The theological convictions of the Reformation are often summarized in terms of a formal principle (Scripture) and a material principle (justification). Form and matter are categories borrowed from Aristotle. Simply put, form signifies the shape or pattern of a particular thing, whereas matter signifies the "stuff" out of which the thing is made. Thus, the formal pattern of reformational doctrine is Scripture, and the material content of reformational doctrine is justification by faith alone.

Summaries of the Reformation often expand upon these two principles to encompass five distinct "cries" of the Reformation, the so-called "five *solas*" of the Reformation:

Sola Scriptura: Scripture alone
Sola fide: Faith alone
Sola gratia: Grace alone

Solus Christus: Christ alone

Soli Deo Gloria: To the glory of God alone[4]

While the Reformers themselves did not summarize their commitments in precisely these terms, the five *solas* summarize well their doctrinal convictions. We will address the last four of these in the next section, but we begin with the source of Protestant convictions in Holy Scripture.

Reformational theology begins with the conviction that Scripture alone is the supreme source of Christian theology. No creed or council, no pope or ecclesiastical body, has the authority to supplant or supplement the final authority of the Bible for Christian belief and practice. To be sure, the definitive revelation of God is embodied in the person of Jesus Christ himself. As the book of Hebrews puts it, "Long ago, at many times and in many ways, God spoke to our fathers by the prophets, but in these last days he has spoken to us by his Son, whom he appointed the heir of all things, through whom he created the world" (Heb 1:1–2 ESV). But we come to know about the person and work of Jesus through the inspired writings of his apostles, and while the revelation of Christ's gospel is manifested apart from the law, as the apostle Paul affirms, the Law and the Prophets nonetheless "bear witness to it" (Rom 3:21 ESV). Thus, the inscripturated Word of God (that is, the Scriptures) provides our fundamental access to and encounter with the incarnate Word of God.

Reformational theology affirms several important attributes of Scripture that are borne out by the Bible's own self-attestation. Most fundamentally, Baptists, along with all orthodox Christians, believe that the Bible is inspired by God. While the Bible is an authentically

---

[4] For a helpful summary of the five *solas*, written by a Baptist church historian, see S. D. Ellison, *Five: The Solas of the Reformation* (Lansville, Australia: Tulip, 2020).

human book—bearing all the marks of its various authors' styles, historical contexts, and languages—it also has its ultimate source in the will of God. All Scripture is "breathed out by God" (2 Tim 3:16 ESV). The authors of Scripture were "carried along by the Holy Spirit" such that they "spoke from God" (2 Pet 1:21). While some of the Bible's language was directly dictated by God himself, the ordinary process of inspiration was more dynamic in nature. The authors wrote what they intended to write (think of the emotionally expressive Psalms or the pastorally specific letters of the New Testament), but the whole process was superintended by the Spirit such that the final product must be received as the very Word of God written.

Because the Bible is inspired by God himself, it is also inerrant and infallible: it does not and cannot err in its properly interpreted intention.[5] Inerrancy does not mean that the Bible is always precise in a scientific or journalistic sense. It includes rounded numbers, approximated speech, generic diversity, and language that is accommodated to human experience. But everything that it affirms is true. When it records truths about the natural world, human history, miraculous events, and moral principles, it comes with the authority and imprimatur of God himself. Scripture, as our Lord teaches, cannot be broken.

Because Scripture is inspired and inerrant, it is also authoritative. It stands over us as the supreme authority for what we are to believe and practice. We are not free to revise its doctrinal and moral teaching. In the words of the Second London Confession, "The authority of the Holy Scripture, for which it ought to be believed, depends not upon the testimony of any man or church, but wholly

[5] For a discussion of Scripture's attributes, including inerrancy and infallibility, see Timothy Ward, *Words of Life: Scripture as the Living and Active Word of God* (Downers Grove: IVP Academic, 2009).

upon God (who is truth itself), the author thereof; therefore it is to be received because it is the Word of God."[6]

The Bible is also sufficient for what we need to know and understand about God in order to inherit eternal life. To be sure, God has revealed himself generally to all humans in creation and conscience by means of common grace. But what we can know about God and the world by nature is always consistent with what we know by grace from Scripture. When it is received by the Spirit's regenerating work, the Bible is clearer and more comprehensive in its teachings than what we can know by nature alone.

The Reformers, and the Baptists after them, also emphasized that the Bible is perspicuous, or clear, in its principal teachings. Not everything in Scripture is equally clear, but what we need to know in order to believe and obey God is clearly revealed to those who make a diligent attempt to understand its truths. As the Second London Baptist Confession puts it:

> All things in Scripture are not alike plain in themselves, nor alike clear unto all; yet those things which are necessary to be known, believed and observed for salvation, are so clearly propounded and opened in some place of Scripture or other, that not only the learned, but the unlearned, in a due use of ordinary means, may attain to a sufficient understanding of them.[7]

In sum, Baptist theology, as reformational, receives the Scriptures of the Old and New Testaments as the only inspired, inerrant, infallible, authoritative, and perspicuous Word of God. Although

---

[6] "The Second London Baptist Confession of Faith," Article 1, in *Baptist Confessions of Faith,* eds. William L. Lumpkin and Billy J.Leonard, 231.

[7] "The Second London Baptist Confession of Faith," Article 1, 233.

some modern Baptists came to question this comprehensive commitment to scriptural authority, the historic Baptist position maintains that everything that the Bible affirms as true is true. This affirmation is foundational to everything that Baptists believe and practice as followers of Jesus Christ. To the degree that we wish to believe and obey Jesus, we must continue to uphold this high view of Scripture, because it is precisely the unbreakable word of God (John 10:35) that bears ongoing witness to the Lord Jesus Christ (John 5:39).

Protestant Soteriology

If Scripture is the formal principle of the Reformation, justification by faith alone is its material principle. The Bible gives shape to reformational theology, and justification provides its distinctive content. But again, this soteriological commitment has been summarized in terms of several exclusive claims.

First, justification is by faith alone (*sola fide*). In its New Testament usage, justification connotes God's forensic, or legal, declaration of ungodly sinners as righteous for the sake of Christ. Jesus Christ in his active and passive obedience is the sole ground of our right standing before God. This legal righteousness is credited, or imputed, to believers in virtue of their union with him, brought about by the work of the Holy Spirit. Faith alone, "receiving and resting" on Christ and his righteousness, is the sole instrument by which believers receive this precious gift.[8] In contradistinction to Roman Catholic theology, when it comes to the reception of justification, good works play no part. Good works inevitably and invariably follow upon true, saving faith, but it is the open hand of faith alone that accepts the gift of justification. As we will see in the following

[8] "The Second London Baptist Confession of Faith," Article 11.2, Lumpkin and Leonard, 255–56.

points, faith itself is not a work and is therefore not meritorious. Justification is sheer divine grace, and Christ alone is its sole ground.

Second, and related, justification is by grace alone (*sola gratia*) and is not the result of human merit. Our good works are never complete or perfect in this life and cannot serve as the basis of our right standing before God. Good works always accompany saving faith as its evidential fruit. Justification is by grace alone through faith alone, "yet is not alone in the person justified, but is ever accompanied with all other saving graces, and is no dead faith, but works by love."[9] This subsequent work of the Holy Spirit, causing believers to grow in holiness, is known as sanctification. Justification and sanctification always go together but are distinct graces in the believer's life. Our confidence can never rest upon our obedience but must always be founded upon the obedience of Christ in his life, death, and resurrection.

Third, Christ alone is the mediator of these mercies. He alone is the Prophet, Priest, and King of the new covenant. No earthly mediator can dispense this divine grace. Only Christ can bridge the gap between a holy God and fallen humanity. Therefore, all believers have confident access to Christ and do not need any other priestly mediator. To be sure, reformational and Baptist theologies have a high view of the church. The church is the people of God, the body and bride of Christ, and the temple of the Holy Spirit. Sinners receive the saving grace of Christ through the church's ministry of Word, sacraments/ordinances, and discipline. But the church is always a servant of the Word, which bears witness to Christ, who is the sole mediator.

Fourth, this rich doctrine of divine grace redounds to the glory of God alone (*Soli Deo Gloria*). Salvation is a work of divine mercy

---

[9] "The Second London Baptist Confession of Faith," Article 11.2, Lumpkin and Leonard, 255–56.

from first to last. From God's election in eternity past, through the saving obedience of Jesus Christ, to the regenerating, indwelling, and preserving work of the Holy Spirit, salvation always belongs to the Lord. God alone deserves all the praise, honor, thanksgiving, and glory for the believer's justification, sanctification, and final glorification.

Baptists, no less than their fellow Protestants, have emphasized these cardinal Reformation truths. The great Baptist confessions affirm that salvation is by grace alone through faith alone in Christ alone on the authority of Scripture alone to the glory of God alone. Baptist theologians such as Benjamin Keach, John Gill, and Andrew Fuller have written in defense of these Protestant principles. Baptist missionaries, preachers, and evangelists such as William Carey, Charles Spurgeon, and Billy Graham have heralded these doctrines of grace as the only hope for human salvation. As we have seen, Baptists are catholic insofar as they affirm the creedal doctrines of the Trinity, the incarnation, and the atonement. But they are also Protestant inasmuch as they have remained committed to the formal and material principles of the Reformation.

CHAPTER 3

Evangelical: Baptists and the Gospel

Introduction

We have been laying the theological foundations for the Baptist vision, but before we proceed to what makes Baptists distinct, we must first explain what makes Baptists Christian. We have seen that Baptists are "catholic" in that they constitute a renewal movement within the universal church. Baptists are followers of Jesus Christ as the definitive revelation of the triune God. This commits us to a belief in the Holy Trinity, the God who is one in essence and three in persons, sharing the same divine nature and distinguished only by their eternal relations of origin. It also commits us to a belief in the incarnation, the astonishing reality that God the Son has assumed true humanity without ceasing to be truly and fully God, and to a belief in the atonement, the reconciling work of Jesus Christ through his whole course of obedience. As noted in the last chapter, Baptists are also "reformational" because they embrace the theological commitments of the Protestant Reformation: sinners are saved by grace alone through faith alone in Christ alone on the basis of Scripture alone to the glory of God alone. In chapter 4, we will transition to theological foundations that issue forth in Baptist distinctives—namely, our "covenantal" hermeneutic. In this chapter, we examine what it means to say that Baptists are "evangelical," a people committed to a particular understanding of how the gospel shapes the Christian life.

Evangelicalism: Preserving an Identity

The moniker "evangelical" has fallen on hard times in many corners of the Western church. In North America, it most commonly connotes something political and sociological. We often hear more about evangelical voters than evangelical churchgoers or theologians. To be sure, evangelical theology has social and cultural implications. Evangelicals, based on biblical convictions, have rightly espoused policies in defense of unborn human life and in favor of traditional marriage and family values. *The Baptist Faith and Message* 2000 expresses Baptist convictions on the Christian's social obligation:

> In the spirit of Christ, Christians should oppose racism, every form of greed, selfishness, and vice, and all forms of sexual immorality, including adultery, homosexuality, and pornography. We should work to provide for the orphaned, the needy, the abused, the aged, the helpless, and the sick. We should speak on behalf of the unborn and contend for the sanctity of all human life from conception to natural death. Every Christian should seek to bring industry, government, and society as a whole under the sway of the principles of righteousness, truth, and brotherly love.[1]

As evangelicals, Baptists are committed to both sound doctrine and social action—not an either/or but a both/and. From our origins, Baptists have been concerned with the social implications of biblical

[1] "XV. The Christian and the Social Order," *The Baptist Faith and Message* 2000, The Southern Baptist Convention, https://bfm.sbc.net/bfm2000/.

teaching. We might consider the Baptist commitment to liberty of conscience and religious freedom (see chapters 5 and 9). We might also think of the great Baptist missionary William Carey and his opposition to the Hindu practice of *sati*, the burning of widows on their husbands' funeral pyres,[2] Andrew Fuller's opposition to the slave trade,[3] the many courageous black Baptists involved in the Civil Rights Movement, or Carl Henry's lifelong pursuit of Christian public engagement.[4] Evangelicalism resists both the cultural retreat and quietism of fundamentalism and the theological liberalism and reductionism of the social gospel.[5] Sound doctrine and social action are integral to the Baptist vision.

---

[2] See Timothy George, *Faithful Witness: The Life and Mission of William Carey* (Birmingham: New Hope, 1991), 149–52.

[3] In his 1803 sermon, "Christian Patriotism," Andrew Fuller states: "To prevent mistakes, however, it is proper to observe that the patriotism required of us is not that love of our country which clashes with universal benevolence, or which seeks its prosperity at the expense of the general happiness of mankind. Such was the patriotism of Greece and Rome; and such is that of all others where Christian principle is not allowed to direct it. Such, I am ashamed to say, is that with which some have advocated the cause of negro slavery. It is necessary, forsooth, to the wealth of this country! No; if my country cannot prosper but at the expense of justice, humanity, and the happiness of mankind, let it be unprosperous! But this is not the case. Righteousness will be found to exalt a nation, and so to be true wisdom." Baptist History Homepage, http://baptisthistoryhomepage.com/fuller.sermon.partiotism.html.

[4] See especially the influential 1947 manifesto, Carl F. H. Henry, *The Uneasy Conscience of Modern Fundamentalism* (Grand Rapids: Eerdmans, 2003).

[5] Fundamentalism means different things to different people. If the term connotes a theologically orthodox Protestantism, one committed to the fundamentals of the faith, then we would happily wear the label. But the term can also describe a particular social and ecclesial posture that is characterized by cultural retreat, anti-intellectualism, legalistic morality, and peculiarities like so-called King James Onlyism and second-degree separation (separation not only from the world but also from Christians deemed insufficiently fundamentalist). In this sense, fundamentalism represents a dangerous tendency, one that post-war evangelicals like Carl Henry and Billy Graham sought to remedy. For more on fundamentalism, see George M. Marsden, *Fundamentalism and American Culture*, 2nd ed. (Oxford: Oxford University Press, 2006). For Henry's programmatic evangelical critique of fundamentalism, see Carl F. H. Henry, *The Uneasy Conscience of Modern Fundamentalism* (Grand Rapids: Eerdmans, 1947).

When evangelicalism becomes co-opted by political powers and reduced to a particular voting bloc, something historically and theologically significant is lost. To many people's minds, "evangelical" is largely synonymous with "white Protestant Republican." Because of these dynamics, some have wondered whether we should jettison the term altogether. But as Baptist historian David Bebbington has observed, the term is no longer the exclusive preserve of Westerners. Evangelicalism is now a global movement, and evangelicals in persecuted contexts often depend upon the label for historical and ecclesiastical legitimacy.[6] Despite the ongoing influence of evangelicals in the West, the center of gravity for evangelicalism is increasingly shifting south and east. Evangelicalism has a rich history, and it now represents a global renewal movement. We should be very hesitant to abandon its patrimony.

As we are using the term here, *evangelical* is a theological and religious phenomenon before it is a social and political phenomenon. As a variety of Protestantism, evangelicalism has its roots in the Protestant Reformation of the sixteenth century (see chapter 2 for those reformational distinctives). But it has also been particularly shaped by several other streams of Anglo-American religiosity: Puritanism, pietism, the evangelical awakenings and revivals of the eighteenth and nineteenth centuries, controversies with modernity, movements of intellectual and cultural renewal in the post-World War II era, and late twentieth-century political dynamics. Evangelicalism represents a vibrant renewal movement within the church, and Baptists have been both active participants in and beneficiaries of its dynamism.

---

[6] Bebbington made these remarks at an event for the Center for Baptist Renewal held on the campus of Oklahoma Baptist University in November 2022.

Evangelical Convictions

The name *evangelical* derives from the Greek term for the gospel: *euangelion*, the evangel, the good news. In chapter 1, we defined the gospel in terms of Jesus Christ himself: the good news that the kingdom of God has come through the incarnation, life, death, burial, and resurrection of Jesus Christ for the salvation of the world. In this sense, the evangel is not the exclusive preserve of evangelicals. All true Christians believe in and proclaim the gospel, which is the power of God for salvation to everyone who believes (Rom 1:16). But evangelicalism marks a particular understanding of this gospel and its implications for Christian life and mission.

The most famous attempt at a theological definition of evangelicalism has been suggested by David Bebbington in his influential *Evangelicalism in Modern Britain: A History from the 1730s to the 1980s*. According to "Bebbington's quadrilateral," evangelicals are marked by a combination of four main theological commitments: "*conversionism*, the belief that lives need to be changed; *activism*, the expression of the gospel in effort; *biblicism*, a particular regard for the Bible; and what may be called *crucicentrism*, a stress on the sacrifice of Christ on the cross. Together they form a quadrilateral of priorities that is the basis of Evangelicalism."[7]

Evangelicalism as a movement is broader than the Baptist denomination. Indeed, some have argued that evangelicalism in its twentieth-century manifestation is something alien to what it means to be a Southern Baptist in particular. Foy Valentine, the moderate executive secretary of the Southern Baptist Christian Life Commission (now the Ethics and Religious Liberty Commission) once told

---

[7] David W. Bebbington, *Evangelicalism in Modern Britain: A History from the 1730s to the 1980s* (London: Routledge, 1988), 2–3.

a reporter: "We are not evangelicals. That's a Yankee word."[8] Still, some of the leading figures among the post-World War II evangelicals were self-consciously Baptist—the theologian Carl F. H. Henry and the evangelist Billy Graham principal among them. Long before the Southern Baptist Convention existed, Baptists were engaged in the movements that formed and shaped evangelicalism. For example, William Carey, the founder of the modern missions movement, was heavily influenced by the Great Awakening preacher Jonathan Edwards. Baptists are arguably the most faithful expression of the evangelical impulse. Our core doctrine of a believers' church is predicated upon the freedom and responsibility of every individual to repent of his sins and believe in the gospel. So, conversionism is very close to the heart of the Baptist vision. Carey and his Baptist compatriots, such as the theologian Andrew Fuller, saw in Edwards's articulation of human free will a theological justification for the free offer of the gospel. Fallen humans are naturally able to respond to God in obedience, though we are morally unable to do so apart from the regenerating grace of God. God may predestine some to everlasting life, but all have a duty to respond to the gospel in repentance and faith.[9]

The converted life issues forth in an active commitment to biblical obedience. As Protestants and evangelicals, Baptists maintain that justification is by faith alone: the ungodly are declared righteous

---

[8] See Collin Hansen and Justin Taylor, "From Babylon Baptist to Baptists in Babylon: The SBC and the Broader Evangelical Community," in *The SBC and the 21st Century: Reflection, Renewal, and Recommitment*, rev. ed., ed. Jason K. Allen (Nashville: B&H Academic, 2019), 33.

[9] William Carey, *Enquiry into the Obligations of Christians to Use Means for the Conversion of the Heathen* (London: Carey Kingsgate, 1961); Andrew Fuller, *Gospel Worthy of All Acceptation*, 3rd ed. (Philadelphia: Charles Cist, 1805). See also Jonathan Edwards, *Freedom of the Will* (London: Hamilton, Adams, and Paternoster, 1860); and Timothy George, *Faithful Witness: The Life and Mission of William Carey* (Birmingham: New Hope, 1991).

before God only for the sake of Christ's obedience, a gift received only through the open hand of faith. Baptist confessions have made clear that true saving faith invariably issues forth in a life of good works. As we will see in chapter 11, one of the hallmarks of the Baptist vision is a commitment to "covenanted holiness": we commit to one another in the context of local assemblies to live lives worthy of the gospel and open to the discipline and correction of the congregation. Baptists are also uniquely committed to a life of mission. As the people of God, the body of Christ, and the temple of the Holy Spirit, the church is by its very nature a missionary people. We are summoned to "come and see" the saving presence of Christ and are then commissioned to invite others to "come and see" his life-giving work (John 1:39, 46). If there was a "life verse" we could apply to the entire Baptist movement, surely it would be the Great Commission of Matt 28:18–20 (ESV):

> And Jesus came and said to them, "All authority in heaven and on earth has been given to me. Go therefore and make disciples of all nations, baptizing them in the name of the Father and of the Son and of the Holy Spirit, teaching them to observe all that I have commanded you. And behold, I am with you always, to the end of the age."

Activism in personal holiness and mission is a core evangelical commitment that Baptists have eagerly embraced.

Likewise, biblicism, a commitment to the supreme authority of Holy Scripture, is also integral to the Baptist vision. As we saw in the previous chapter, Baptists are uniquely committed to the supremacy of the Bible over all ecclesiastical authorities, whether episcopal or confessional. Baptists have been prolific in producing confessions of faith, which have been utilized as instruments of unity and accountability, both at the local church level and the associational level.[10] Baptist have remained committed to the creedal foundations of Christianity (see chapter 1), but confessions of faith are seen in the Baptist tradition as more readily revisable than in more rigidly confessional denominations. It has not been uncommon for pastors and local churches to craft their own confessions of faith in order to summarize their biblical commitments. The Bible alone is the supreme litmus test for Christian faithfulness, and theological formulation primarily takes place through biblical exegesis (though certainly informed by traditional interpretations, as we see in the Baptist luminary John Gill, who made copious references to church fathers and Reformation-era teachers).

Finally, crucicentrism has also been a key mark of the Baptist movement as an expression of evangelicalism. Though Baptist theologians have developed differing models of the atonement and have disagreed on its extent (general vs. particular), no one can deny the central place of the cross of Jesus Christ in the Baptist vision. The church's mission is to make disciples of Jesus Christ primarily by proclaiming his atoning death and victorious resurrection. The remarks attributed to the great nineteenth-century Baptist preacher, Charles Haddon Spurgeon, are indicative: "I take my text and make a beeline to the cross."[11] The cross is the central event in the drama of redemption, and it occupies a singular place in Baptist preaching and discipleship.

---

[10] See Lumpkin and Leonard, ed., *Baptist Confessions of Faith*. On the congregational and associational use of confessional symbols, see Greg Wills, *Democratic Religion: Freedom, Authority, and Church Discipline in the Baptist South*, 1785–1900 (Oxford: Oxford University Press, 1997).

[11] Spurgeon admirers have had a difficult time finding this precise phrase in his writings, but the sentiment certainly expresses his approach. And it is one that we heartily commend.

Bebbington's quadrilateral has sometimes been critiqued and supplemented by other evangelicals. Fellow Baptist historian Thomas Kidd suggests that the presence of the Holy Spirit is also a defining mark of evangelicalism, and the growth of the Pentecostal wing of evangelicalism gives further evidence for its inclusion.[12] For their part, Baptists have been eager to emphasize the role of the Spirit in bringing about regeneration and in indwelling, empowering, and preserving the followers of Christ.[13] Other distinguishing marks of evangelicals might be added as well, but Bebbington's list and Kidd's revisions seem sufficient to summarily mark out what it means to be an evangelical. As we have seen, Baptists have been at the forefront of this renewal movement.

---

[12] Thomas S. Kidd, *Who Is an Evangelical? The History of a Movement in Crisis* (New Haven: Yale University Press, 2019).

[13] See "II. God," *The Baptist Faith and Message* 2000, The Southern Baptist Convention, https://bfm.sbc.net/bfm2000/#ii.

CHAPTER 4

Covenantal: The Baptist Hermeneutic

What we have said so far about Baptist identity does not distinguish us much from other Christians, especially other Protestants. However, the Baptist understanding of the relation between the covenants is truly our defining theological commitment. Our covenantal hermeneutic influences everything from liberty of conscience to believers' baptism and covenantal Communion to the autonomy of the local church and religious liberty. It truly is the foundation of Baptist theology and practice.

The Biblical Storyline, the Inauguration of the New Covenant, and Baptist Identity

At creation, the triune God created all that is and ordered it according to his purposes. Namely, he made creation to center on his people—Adam and Eve, human beings created in his image—dwelling with him in his place—the land, the garden of Eden (Gen 1:26–28). As God's image bearers and his representatives on Earth, Adam and Eve were to perform specific tasks given by God. They were to be fruitful and multiply God's image bearers (Gen 1:28), exercise dominion (or rule) over God's place (Gen 1:26, 28), cultivate and keep God's dwelling place with them (Gen 2:15), and obey God's Word (Gen 2:16–17). Rather than fulfilling these tasks, however,

Adam and Eve listened to the voice of the serpent, the enemy, and sinned against God by disobeying his word (Gen 3:1–13). In their rebellion, they failed to rule as well. Because of their rebellion, their ability to be fruitful and to cultivate and keep God's dwelling place became difficult and burdensome.

God responded to humanity's rebellion with both judgment and mercy (Gen 3:14–24). In judgment, God multiplied the woman's pain during childbearing and made it exceedingly difficult for the man to bring forth good fruit from the ground. He also cast them from his presence, exiling them out of the garden. But in his mercy, he did not utterly destroy them; rather, he clothed them and promised that one day the seed of woman would come and destroy the serpent, reversing the curse of Adam and restoring what Adam lost (Gen 3:15). To quote the last verse of "Joy to the World," one day someone will come and redeem the world "far as the curse is found."[1]

The rest of the Old Testament can be summarized as a search for this seed of woman. In Genesis, we learn that God will bring the seed from the line of Abraham, Isaac, and Jacob. God promises to Abraham that he will give Abraham good land to dwell in, many kings from his line, and descendants that will outnumber the stars in the sky or the sands on the seashore (Gen 12:1–3; 15:5–7; 17:4–14). In other words, God promised to restore what Adam lost through a descendant of Abraham, Isaac, and Jacob. And indeed, their descendants multiply and become the nation of Israel. God brought them out of slavery in Egypt, through the blood of the lamb and the death of the firstborn son (Exodus 1–15), and took them to the Promised Land, the land flowing with milk and honey (Exodus 16–Joshua 5). There, God continued to multiply them, they ate from the abundance of the land, they eventually received a king from God, David, who

[1] Isaac Watts, "Joy to the World," accessed June 18, 2024, https://hymnary.org/text/joy_to_the_world_the_lord_is_come.

ruled over God's place (1 Samuel 16), and David's son, Solomon, built a temple for the Lord in which he dwelled with his people (2 Chronicles 3–9). From one vantage point, God's promises to Abraham seem to be fulfilled.

But these were shadows of the fulfillment that was still to come after the end of the Old Testament. The temple had been destroyed and rebuilt to a lesser degree of glory (2 Kings 25), Israel had been exiled, and there was no king ruling over God's people. In spite of the apparent restoration of God's original purposes for Adam and Eve—kings, the temple or tabernacle, the Promised Land, and the multiplication of God's people—Israel continually failed to obey God. From the patriarchs' various failures, to Israel's obstinance at the Red Sea, at Sinai, and in the wilderness, to their idolatry during the conquest, to David's and Solomon's various egregious sins during their reigns at the height of Israel's success, Israel refused to obey God's word and was cast from his presence just like Adam. At the end of the Old Testament, we are left waiting for the seed of woman to come, reverse the curse, and restore what Adam had lost. We are left wondering when God will send his Spirit, the only person who can help his people finally obey God's word.

Before jumping to the inauguration of the new covenant and the coming of the seed of woman, we need to explore the nature of the old covenant a bit more. God's covenant with Abraham included every physical descendant of Abraham and Sarah as his covenant people. In other words, entry into the old covenant was not by faith but by physical birth, and circumcision was a purely physical sign of this covenant (Genesis 17). The law given at Sinai and again on the plains of Moab governed both the spiritual and social life of Israel, but not all Israel was faithful to those laws. This is, in part, because they were a "mixed body," made up of both believers and unbelievers. The promise of the new covenant in Jeremiah 31 or

Ezekiel 36–37 is that one day when the seed comes, he will pour his Spirit onto all those included in the new covenant so that they can finally obey. In the meantime, God will whittle his people down to a remnant, even down to a single person, the Stump of Jesse (Isaiah 9, 11). That one person will bring about the new covenant and all the promises contained therein.

When Jesus came, he fulfilled all these new covenant promises. He is the Davidic King who defeated Israel's (and the world's) enemies—namely, sin and death. He is the faithful Israelite who obeyed completely. He is the Passover Lamb, slain for the sins of the world, who descended into death and rose from the dead in victory over death. He is the Temple of God, God the Son who came in the flesh and dwelled among us (John 1:14). He renewed and restored the land through his miracles and ultimately through the new creation he inaugurated by his resurrection from the dead. He is, in other words, the seed of woman who crushed the serpent's head, and the son of David and Abraham who fulfilled all God's promises to Israel in himself (2 Cor 1:20).

Because Jesus is the one man, the God-man, who fulfilled God's promises to Israel (and thus to the world), he is Israel. All who are united to him by faith are now part of the covenant people of God, the new Israel, made up of both Jews and Gentiles. Entrance into the covenant people is no longer by physical birth but by faith—spiritual new birth. Jesus makes this abundantly clear in John 3:5–7 (ESV):

> Truly, truly, I say to you, unless one is born of water and the Spirit, he cannot enter the kingdom of God. That which is born of the flesh is flesh, and that which is born of the Spirit is spirit. Do not marvel that I said to you, "You must be born again."

This is the fundamental change that occurs in the new covenant. Likewise, the sign of the covenant changed from a physical sign, circumcision, to a spiritual sign, baptism. While the latter sign is still material, it also transcends its physical reality to signify a spiritual movement of the baptized person from spiritual death to new, eternal life in Christ. The same is not true of circumcision. The Old Testament makes this distinction when it says that in the new covenant the people of God will receive the circumcision of the heart rather than of the flesh (Deut 10:12–17; Jer 4:4; cf. Rom 2:25–29). The nature of these two covenants is different; the old covenant is a shadow of the new covenant, and its physical, local realities (entry by birth, the Promised Land, the kings, national boundaries, etc.) point forward to the spiritual and global realities bought by the person and work of Jesus.

Different Types of Baptist Covenantalism

Baptists have articulated this relation between the covenants in various ways. For many Baptists and baptistic evangelicals beginning in the nineteenth century, *dispensational theology* has provided the basic framework for thinking about the biblical covenants. The primary emphasis in dispensationalism is placed upon discontinuity between Old Testament Israel and the New Testament church.[2] These two dispensations do not represent different systems of salvation (works vs. faith), but they do mark out two distinct peoples of God: ethnic, geopolitical Israel and the predominantly Gentile church. In dispensational theology, the promises made to Israel in the Old Testament must have literal fulfillments for Israel as a nation-state.

[2] For an introduction to dispensationalism that attempts to be both charitable and critical, see Brian Irwin and Tim Perry, *After Dispensationalism: Reading the Bible for the End of the World* (Bellingham: Lexham, 2023).

The distinctives of this system include a pre-tribulational rapture of the church, a literal seven-year tribulation, and a literal thousand-year reign of Christ on Earth following his Second Coming and before the final judgment. Even within dispensationalism, there are variations between classic dispensationalism, modified dispensationalism, and progressive dispensationalism (with the last variety making more room for the already-not-yet inauguration of Christ's kingdom). But each of these perspectives tends to make a rather sharp distinction between Israel and the church.

The early Baptists, however, did not rely on this system, which was only fully developed in the nineteenth century. Instead, they tended to espouse a form of *covenant* or *federal theology*. In this system, there are three primary covenants contained in the biblical revelation. First, there is the eternal covenant of redemption, or covenant of peace, in which the persons of the Trinity agreed to accomplish the salvation of the elect through the incarnation and atoning death of the Son. Baptists such as John Gill appealed to texts such as Isa 54:10 and Zech 6:13 to underscore this eternal, intratrinitarian decree.[3] Second, there is the covenant of works that God established with Adam in Eden (Hos 6:7), promising life and warning of death, depending on his obedient response to the divine command. Acting as a representative (or covenant head) of his posterity, Adam broke this covenant and so rightly merited condemnation for all who descended from him by ordinary generation. Thus, a third covenant was revealed to Adam: the covenant of grace. Reformed paedobaptists argued that the covenant of grace was established in each of the post-fall biblical covenants (Noahic, Abrahamic, Mosaic, Davidic, and New). For these theologians, the covenant of grace is one in substance, though

---

[3] See John Gill, *A Complete Body of Doctrinal and Practical Divinity,* 2 vols. (Grand Rapids: Baker, 1978), 1:20.

distinct in administration. This strict continuity of the covenant of grace undergirds the continuing practice of infant baptism—just as believers and their children in the old covenant received the covenant sign of circumcision, so also believers and their children in the new covenant are to receive the covenant sign of baptism. The early Baptists obviously rejected this application of covenant theology. Instead, they tended to view the covenant of grace as promised in Old Testament—as early as Gen 3:15—and revealed in a progressive way through the various covenants. But the covenant of grace was only formally established in the new covenant which was enacted by Christ's incarnation, suffering, and glorification. Thc Old Testament saints were saved on the basis of the new covenant, which was mediated through the Old Testament covenants, but only the new covenant is to be identified with the covenant of grace itself.[4]

In recent decades, some Baptists have sought to chart a middle course between dispensational theology and Reformed covenant theology. There is a family of views that fall under this rubric. *New covenant theology* tends to reject the threefold covenantal arrangement in classic covenant theology (covenant of redemption, covenant of works, and covenant of grace). Instead, these Baptist interpreters focus on the historical biblical covenants themselves and argue for the discontinuity of the new covenant from the Old Testament covenants, but without the dispensational scheme related to Israel.[5] Others have developed a view known as *progressive*

---

[4] For a recent defense of Baptist covenant theology, see Samuel Renihan, *The Mystery of Christ, His Covenant, and His Kingdom* (Cape Coral, FL: Founders, 2019). There are variations even within Baptist covenant theology, but those distinctions need not detain us. For another perspective, see Earl Blackburn, *It Pleased the Lord to Make a Covenant of Grace: A Critique of 1689 Federalism* (Elkin, NC: Veritas Heritage, 2023).

[5] See Tom Wells and Fred Zaspel, *New Covenant Theology: Description, Definition, Defense* (New Covenant Media, 2002).

covenantalism, which similarly treats the historical biblical covenants as progressively revealing the new covenant, accounting for both continuity and discontinuity.[6] In places where Baptist covenant theology emphasizes continuity (for example, the abiding normativity of the Decalogue, including its sabbatarian demands), progressive covenantalism stresses discontinuity (arguing that the Sabbath command was fulfilled and abrogated in the new covenant).

It is not our aim to adjudicate between these varieties within the Baptist tradition. There are important differences, but on the question of the constitution of the new covenant people of God, there is agreement. The shift from the Old Testament covenants to the new covenant signals a shift in the makeup of the covenant community, which has deep implications for Baptist ecclesiology. Since only those who are rightly related to Jesus Christ by faith are members of the new covenant, and only these are to be admitted to church membership, the visible church is to be composed of believers only. Therefore, the sacraments are reserved for believers only. Baptism does not bring the infant children of believers into the new covenant but is only a sign and seal of covenant membership to those who are truly converted. The church recognizes these by their willful and credible profession of faith, regardless of age. Baptists still raise their children in the nurture and admonition of the Lord, they still teach them to pray, and they still catechize them in Christian doctrine. But the confirming rite of baptism is reserved for those who credibly profess faith in Jesus Christ.[7]

---

[6] For the definitive exposition of this approach, see Peter J. Gentry and Stephen J. Wellum, *Kingdom through Covenant: A Biblical-Theological Understanding of the Covenants*, 2nd ed. (Wheaton: Crossway, 2018).

[7] We are grateful for the feedback and suggestions of Garrett Walden in clarifying the various perspectives. Any missteps in the final version are ours alone.

Conclusion: Baptist Covenantalism and Baptist Distinctives

For all of these options, there is a distinct change from the old covenant to the new covenant. As we will see in subsequent chapters, this Baptist hermeneutic, based on a particular understanding of the relation between the old and new covenants, gives rise to Baptist theology and practice as it pertains to baptism, Communion, polity, and the role of the state. Because of the shift from the old covenant to the new covenant, and especially the change in manner of entry from birth to faith, the sign of the covenant is only for those who enter by faith and thus not given at birth. The covenant meal, Communion, is only for those who have entered into the covenant by faith and subsequently received the covenant sign. The covenant people of God, each individually indwelt by the Spirit, govern themselves under the lordship of Christ, rather than being governed by some higher human authority. And the church governs spiritual matters, rather than the state governing both the devotional and the social life of its citizens. We will explore each of these distinctives in the next section. This understanding of the change from the old covenant to the new covenant dictates every theological and practical distinctive of the Baptist tradition.

PART II

DISTINCTIVES

CHAPTER 5

Liberty of Conscience

To this point, we have sought to lay the theological foundations of the Baptist vision. Baptists are catholic, reformational, evangelical, and covenantal. We now turn our attention to the distinctive beliefs that flow from the last of these foundations. At the risk of oversimplification, we maintain that the most fundamental Baptist distinctive is that each individual person is responsible before God under the supreme lordship of Jesus Christ. No church, political state, family member, or other person can represent the individual before God and speak on his or her behalf. Each individual person is responsible for both his or her response to God's offer of salvation in Jesus Christ and the exercise of his or her own membership in the body of Christ, for those who believe. This leads to what we know as Baptist distinctives, and namely: believers' baptism, congregational governance of the local church, and religious freedom. We will discuss each of these and more in the following chapters. But in this chapter, we must begin at the root: liberty of conscience.

Theological Contexts

Baptist emphasis on the liberty of an individual's conscience arises from a number of shared theological commitments with other Christians and, more fundamentally, specific Bible verses. While these verses are acknowledged by other Christians, Baptists claim to apply these verses consistently with those theological commitments to their fullest extent. The most important of these theological commitments is that all human beings are created in God's image.

The *imago dei* signifies a few different but complementary things in Genesis 1 and throughout the rest of the Bible, including the tasks given to Adam and Eve and their status as God's representatives on earth. Another aspect of the image of God is that it dignifies human beings even beyond the ordinary dignity possessed by all of God's creatures. Humans are the pinnacle of God's creation, the climax and center of it. They are uniquely made in God's image, both for the functions they are to perform and because of the kind of relationship they can have with God. In contrast to so-called lower life forms (animals, plants, etc.), humans can, along with angels, hear from and speak to God. In distinction from angels, humans alone can be restored to right relationship with God after the fall through the person and work of Jesus.

In other words, the fact that humans are made in the image of God means, in part, that they are uniquely able to relate to God in their communication with him, their salvation by him, and their representation of him to the rest of creation. What makes humans "human," both corporately and individually, is their relationship to God. This is an important and fundamental point when discussing liberty of conscience. Each individual human being is who he or she is because of his or her individual possession of the image of God and individual relationship to God. No other creature can hear from or speak to God, respond to Jesus in repentance and faith, or obey God's commands.

Someone might object on two related grounds that in the Bible one person can and does stand for others. The first instance is in Genesis 3, when Adam's choice plunges all of humanity into sin.

The second instance is in the Gospels when Jesus's own life and atoning work in his death, descent, and resurrection are applied to those who turn to him in repentance and faith. In the case of the first Adam, we are not only sinners by nature (i.e., through Adam's sin; see Rom 5:12–14) but also by choice (e.g., Rom 3:23; Jer 31:29–30). In the second instance, it is only those who consciously turn to Christ in repentance and faith who receive the saving benefits of his work. In both cases—fallenness and imputed righteousness—it is still ultimately the individual person who stands responsible for their status before God. Liberty of conscience is not a denial of representation but an affirmation of responsibility for each individual, including the responsibility to decide under whose representation they stand—the first Adam's or the last.

This brings us to a second related theological context for liberty of conscience, namely, the doctrine of salvation. For Baptists, a person's standing before God does not change from condemned sinner to justified saint until that person responds publicly in repentance from their sin and faith in Christ's finished work. This is different from other Christian traditions, most of which, albeit in slightly different ways, affirm that a person's status changes before God when they are baptized as an infant. We have already discussed how Baptist theology differs from paedobaptist traditions on the issue of covenant, specifically with respect to how a person is included in the new covenant. The doctrine of salvation is another angle for addressing this issue of liberty of conscience. For Baptists, individuals are not included in God's covenantal people by birth (as with Old Testament Israel) or infant baptism (as with other Christian traditions) but by conscious profession of faith.

No one can stand in for another person with respect to covenantal inclusion. To address it from a personal angle, I cannot be included in God's covenant people simply through someone else representing me. This brings us to a third theological context for liberty of conscience: the doctrine of the church. Entrance into the covenant people of God is not something that happens because I have believing parents who baptize me (as with paedobaptist traditions) or because I have parents who are genetic descendants of Abraham (as with Old Testament Israel). Instead, entrance into Christ's body happens because I profess Christ and him crucified and follow him in baptism. To put it like Jesus does, "unless one is born again he cannot see the kingdom of God" (John 3:3 ESV). Similarly, Paul says in Rom 9:6–8 (ESV),

> For not all who are descended from Israel belong to Israel, and not all are children of Abraham because they are his offspring, but "Through Isaac shall your offspring be named." This means that it is not the children of the flesh who are the children of God, but the children of the promise are counted as offspring.

Liberty of conscience arises from these theological contexts, specifically their relation to a Baptist understanding of the covenants. Because entry into the new covenant comes by faith and not by birth, each individual person is responsible for his or her own status before God in the face of Jesus Christ. Entrance into the new covenant requires each individual to respond to Jesus in repentance and faith and to follow him in baptism.

Biblical Texts

These theological contexts are fundamentally rooted in biblical texts. With respect to God's judgment of sinful humanity, the Bible emphasizes that God deals with each of us according to our own works. Rev 20:12–13 (ESV), for instance, describes the final judgment like this:

> And I saw the dead, great and small, standing before the throne, and books were opened. Then another book was opened, which is the book of life. And the dead were judged by what was written in the books, according to what they had done. And the sea gave up the dead who were in it, Death and Hades gave up the dead who were in them, and they were judged, each one of them, according to what they had done.

Each person is judged here "according to what they had done." For those who are saved, they are judged according to Christ's works, which have been imputed to them by the Spirit through faith. That still puts the onus on the individual to respond to Christ in faith in order to receive the benefits of salvation. In either case, the individual is judged according to his or her own choices. This is why Baptists emphasize liberty of conscience, because in Scripture our relationship to God is a matter of how we each respond to him.

Another important set of biblical texts related to liberty of conscience are those that describe followers of God responding to governmental authorities. In Daniel 6, King Darius issues an edict declaring that his citizens cannot petition any other god in prayer. Daniel responds by praying as he normally does (Dan 6:10), modeling for us the importance of obeying God rather than government when the latter attempts to coerce us into sinful choices. A similar attitude is modeled and expressed in Acts 4–5 by the apostles in the early days of the church, and famously culminates with Peter declaring that "we must obey God rather than men" (Acts 5:29 ESV).

Finally, both James and Paul indicate that a person stands on his or her own two feet, so to speak, with respect to judgment. In Jas 4:12, James says, "There is only one lawgiver and judge who is able to save and to destroy. But who are you to judge your neighbor?" He makes two points here: God is the only judge, and we do not stand in judgment over our neighbor. Judgment and salvation are between each individual and God, and the difference between judgment and salvation is the individual person's response to Jesus Christ. In a related passage, Paul says, "Who are you to pass judgment on the servant of another? It is before his own master that he stands or falls. And he will be upheld, for the Lord is able to make him stand" (Rom 14:4 ESV). Again, each individual person is responsible to their own master, ultimately God himself. We do not stand in judgment over one another but only stand to receive judgment from God.

Liberty of Conscience and Baptist Distinctives

These theological contexts and cited Bible verses are not ignored or downplayed by other Christian traditions. Liberty of conscience is not an exclusively Baptist claim, and credobaptist and paedobaptist traditions alike affirm it. What makes liberty of conscience such a fundamental commitment for Baptists is its importance in our history, in particular at the beginning of the Baptist movement, and how we connect it to our understanding of the relation between the biblical covenants and the issues of baptism, local church governance, and religious liberty.

Regarding our history and heritage, there are a number of important moments in the earliest decades of Baptist history that prompted our emphasis on liberty of conscience. John Smyth's immigration from England to Holland was prompted predominantly by opposition from the British government toward Separatists.

Having been convinced of believers' baptism in 1609, he led his congregation to the Netherlands, where they fellowshipped with a congregation of Waterlander Mennonites and were eventually baptized. One of Smyth's congregants, Thomas Helwys, differed with Smyth on a number of important theological points, mostly having to do with what we would now call distinctions between Baptist and Anabaptist beliefs. Because of those differences, Helwys and a few others left Holland and went back to England. Helwys wrote what is most likely the earliest Baptist defense of religious liberty, "A Short Declaration of the Mistery [sic] of Iniquity," which he published shortly after his return to England in 1612. In it, he criticized current practice of all varieties of English churches, from Roman Catholic to Puritan, and he also gave a biblical and theological defense of liberty of conscience, in relation to the concept of religious liberty, that was rooted in a distinctively Baptist interpretation of Scripture. He was arrested almost immediately after returning from the Netherlands, and it is possible that by sending his treatise to King James I, he had prompted that governmental action.[1] Helwys died in prison four years later.

Helwys, a General (non-Calvinistic) Baptist, was not the only British Baptist to argue for liberty of conscience in the first century of Baptist life. Other General Baptists like Thomas Monck and Thomas Grantham included robust definitions of liberty of conscience, in relation to religious liberty in particular, in their confessions of faith, as did Particular (Calvinistic) Baptists in the seventeenth century.[2] The latter includes Article 21 of the Second

---

[1] On the Smyth and Helwys story, and especially for the description of Helwys's return to England, see Chute, Finn, and Haykin, *The Baptist Story* (Nashville: B&H Academic, 2015), 19–20.

[2] See Articles XLV and XLVI of "The Orthodox Creed," of which Monck was the principal author. The text can be found in Lumpkin and Leonard, ed., *Baptist Confessions of Faith*, 343–45.

London Baptist Confession, of which the opening line of paragraph 2 is perhaps the most famous Baptist slogan regarding liberty of conscience:

> God alone is Lord of the conscience, and has left it free from the doctrines and commandments of men which are in any thing contrary to his word, or not contained in it. So that to believe such doctrines, or obey such commands out of conscience, is to betray true liberty of conscience; and the requiring of an implicit faith, an absolute and blind obedience, is to destroy liberty of conscience and reason also.[3]

Liberty of conscience was a fundamental Baptist belief in the earliest days of Baptist life and thought precisely because it was connected to both their ecclesial and political circumstances and also to their distinctive brand of covenantalism.

This brings us to our second point regarding the fundamental nature of liberty of conscience with respect to Baptist distinctives, namely the connection between liberty of conscience and Baptist covenantalism. We have already discussed the Baptist understanding of the biblical covenants in an earlier chapter, and we will discuss baptism, local church governance, and religious liberty in the following chapters. In this chapter, we have simply demonstrated that liberty of conscience is the connective tissue between these various topics. If, as Baptists argue, the biblical covenants are structured in such a way that with the new covenant there is a change in how one enters into the covenant people of God, from entering by birth to entering by faith, then this is bolstered by all we have said

[3] "The Second London Baptist Confession of Faith," in *Baptist Confessions of Faith*, ed. Lumpkin and Leonard, 275–76.

so far about liberty of conscience. Entrance into the covenant is a matter of liberty of conscience, for each individual must enter or refuse to enter by their own choice and not by birth into a "covenant family." Consequently, the sign of the new covenant, baptism, ought only to be given to those who have entered into that new covenant by conscious profession of faith, rather than by birth into a "covenant family." With respect to religious liberty, governments ought to give its citizens the freedom to exercise their liberty of conscience when it comes to belief and practice.

But it is not just at the level of the individual that Baptists emphasize liberty of conscience; just as Christ alone is Lord of the conscience, so Christ alone is Lord of the (local) church. The same principles apply with respect to local church governance. Each congregation is responsible before the Lord for their own decisions, which means that no one church or bishop or synod or other individual or group can stand over a particular local church.

Conclusion

Liberty of conscience is the most fundamental of all Baptist distinctives; it arises from our understanding of the relation between the biblical covenants and gives shape to our other distinctives—baptism, local church governance, and religious liberty. It is to these other distinctives, along with Communion, that we now turn.

CHAPTER 6

Believers' Baptism

Baptists are named for their most well-known distinctive: believers' baptism. Unfortunately, in many contemporary contexts, Baptist churches often talk mainly about what baptism is not rather than what baptism actually is. In many Baptist churches, baptism may be pushed to a different service other than the normal corporate gathering, or awkwardly tacked on to a service (the same often happens with the Lord's Supper). It might be brief and without much fanfare. And, very often, it is nearly explained away, with those performing a baptism beginning with words like, "this is just water, not magic; there's nothing happening here!"

One might wonder why Baptists even go forward with the baptism after it has been pushed aside, minimized, and explained away. The answer is often simply, "because Jesus commanded it." This is reason enough to continue to perform baptisms. If Jesus commanded it, we ought to follow his instructions. But Jesus's instruction was not arbitrarily given as a random rite to perform to signify one person's decision to follow him. The earliest Baptists believed that baptism signified much more than just a believer's initial step of obedience. They also believed that the *baptizand* (the person being baptized) is not the actor on the stage in the drama of baptism: the confirming church and God himself are also active participants in the ordinance. The early Baptists believed these things because, like good Baptists, they found them in Scripture. In this chapter, we want to explore what the Bible says about baptism and how Baptists incorporate that teaching into their own distinctive beliefs about the proper subjects of baptism. We begin with this fundamental understanding of the ordinance: baptism as a covenant sign and seal for professing believers.

Baptism as Covenant Sign and Seal

In the New Testament, the sign of the covenant shifts from circumcision to baptism. This shift in symbols is itself symbolic of the inauguration of the new covenant in the person and work of Jesus Christ. In the old covenant, entry into the covenant people of God was by birth into the Abrahamic lineage. Those who were born into Jewish families were part of the covenant people of God, the nation of Israel. This boundary for covenantal inclusion was signified by circumcision of every male child. Proselytes—Gentiles who attached themselves to Israel—would often be circumcised as well, but the boundary marker was inclusion in the nation of Israel.

In the new covenant, because of Jesus's life and work, both Jew and Gentile can be included in the church, God's covenant people. The church is not a replacement of Israel but includes all those united to Israel's Messiah, Jesus Christ, God the Son in the flesh. Jesus is the fulfillment of all God's promises to Israel and is himself the descendant of both Abraham and David. Because he is the "True Israel," all those united to him by faith are part of the new Israel that he constitutes around himself. He is also the Second Adam, such that all who are united to him by faith are part of the new humanity. In this way, the church is not a replacement of Israel but the fulfillment of its purpose to be a light to the nations.

This covenantal shift from geopolitical Israel to the church explains the shift in the application of the covenant sign.[1] In the old covenant, entry into the covenant people was by birth, and the sign of the covenant reflected that reality in various ways. In the new covenant, entry into the covenant people is by new birth, or faith, and the covenant sign signifies this reality. The Old Testament itself prophesies of a day when the external sign of circumcision would become an internal reality for the entire covenant community: "And no longer shall each one teach his neighbor and each his brother, saying, 'Know the LORD,' for they shall all know me, from the least of them to the greatest, declares the LORD. For I will forgive their iniquity, and I will remember their sin no more" (Jer 31:34 ESV). Baptism reflects the truth that the entire new covenant community has become the recipient of this promise. Each baptized person has had the law written on his or her heart, died to the old self, and been raised to new life in Christ.

Baptism is the covenant sign and seal, the symbol of entry into the new covenant people of God (the church, or, the new Israel), given to anyone who has been united to Christ by faith.[2] It is a visible proclamation that the person being baptized has forsaken his or her earthly attachments and chosen to give his or her allegiance to Jesus. It also confirms this reality to the person baptized. While faith and repentance are prerequisite to baptism, it is a mistake to think that baptism does nothing. It is God's confirmation to the believer, through the affirmation of the church, that he or she is God's beloved

---

[1] See Stephen J. Wellum, "Baptism and the Relationship between the Covenants," in *Believer's Baptism: Sign of the New Covenant in Christ*, ed. Thomas R. Schreiner and Shawn D. Wright (Nashville: B&H Academic, 2006), 97–161.

[2] On the meaning of baptism (and the Lord's Supper) as a symbol, and on the early Baptist understanding of the ordinances as "sacraments," see Michael A. G. Haykin, *Amidst Us Our Beloved Stands: Recovering Sacrament in the Baptist Tradition* (Bellingham: Lexham, 2022).

child through faith in Jesus. This is the reality foreshadowed by Israel's rite of circumcision. Circumcision signified that Israel was set apart to God. It signaled Israel's allegiance to God and its corollary commitment to refuse the kings and "gods" of the nations. But external circumcision was always meant to foreshadow the circumcision of the heart (Deut 30:6), which would become universalized in the covenant community only with the arrival of the new covenant (Jer 31:34). Baptism signifies Christians' allegiance to God, their submission to him as King, their denial of all other principalities and powers, their death to the sin in which they once walked and by which they were once held captive, and their resurrection to new life in Christ. The person baptized has left the kingdom of darkness and become a citizen of the kingdom of God. Ultimately, each of these movements is simply entry into the new covenant people of God: the church.

Baptism as Spirit-Led Sacrament

Because baptism is a sign of the gospel, outwardly sealing the sinner's movement from death to life through faith in the finished work of Jesus, the church throughout history has seen fit to refer to it as a sacrament. The early Baptists used this same language and did not see *sacrament* and *ordinance* as competing terms. The choice of *ordinance* in early Baptist confessions of faith was not meant to diminish the significance of baptism but to highlight that it stood alongside other ordinances or means of grace ordained by the Lord himself, including the Word, the Lord's Supper, and prayer.[3] The

[3] For an excellent treatment of early Baptist sacramental theology, see Haykin, *Amidst Us Our Beloved Stands*. See also Stanley K. Fowler, *More than a Symbol: The British Baptist Recovery of Baptismal Sacramentalism* (Eugene, OR: Wipf & Stock, 2002).

earliest Baptists (like Benjamin Keach) did not hold to a merely symbolic understanding of baptism, but neither did they believe that baptism was regenerative. Saving faith is prerequisite to baptism, but baptism serves as a public confirmation and proclamation of the believer's new life in Christ. While many modern-day Baptists tend to be suspicious of the term *sacrament* primarily due to latent fears about Roman Catholicism, the earliest Baptists did not share that suspicion. Instead, they used the term to convey the idea that the Lord is indeed active in baptism (and in the Lord's Supper), confirming and strengthening the faith of believers and assuring them through the sign that they are indeed partakers of the thing signified. Through these sacraments, God is actively present with his people through his Word and Spirit. Baptists did not believe that baptism was the cause of their regeneration, nor that baptism was absolutely necessary for salvation. But they did believe that baptism was the "ordinary means of grace" by which the whole conversion process (including hearing, repenting, believing, receiving the Spirit, and publicly identifying with Jesus) was sealed and confirmed.[4] In the New Testament, baptism is closely associated with the forgiveness of sins (Acts 2:38), washing away of sins (Acts 22:16), dying and rising in Christ (Rom 6:1–4), and salvation itself (1 Pet 3:21). Other New Testament texts indicate that the recipients of baptism have already repented, believed, received justification, and (in some instances) even received the baptism of the Holy Spirit (see Acts 10:44–48). We cannot pit these biblical texts against one another. Baptists synthesize this biblical material by maintaining that saving faith is the prerequisite to baptism, and baptism is the ordinary way that new life in Christ is sealed, confirmed, and communicated to the

[4] Robert H. Stein, "Baptism in Luke-Acts," in *Believer's Baptism: Sign of the New Covenant in Christ*, ed. Thomas R. Schreiner and Shawn D. Wright (Nashville: B&H Academic, 2006), 75.

new believer. The early Baptist confessions spoke of baptism, along with Christ's other ordinances: "the outward and ordinary means whereby Christ communicateth to us the benefits of redemption are his ordinances, especially the word, baptism, the Lord's supper, and prayer; all which means are made effectual to the elect for salvation."[5]

Likewise, the seventeenth-century Baptist pastor and theologian Benjamin Keach beautifully describes how the sacraments are used by God to confirm the faith of believers:

> As the Sacrament of the Lord's Supper was ordained to hold forth the breaking of Christ's Body, and the pouring forth of his Blood; So in like manner the Sacrament of Baptism was instituted and appointed to hold forth Christ was really dead, buried, and that he arose again for our Justification. And that this is so, we shall not only prove it from the plain Authority of God's Word, but by the joint Testimony of almost all famous Writers and Divines we have met with, Ancient or Modern. And indeed we cannot but be much affected with the great Love and Goodness of our Blessed Saviour in the Institution of these two great Ordinances, it being his gracious Design and Condescension, hereby to hold forth, or preach, as I may say, to the very sight of our visible Eyes by these fit and proper Mediums, the glorious Doctrine of his Death, Burial, and Resurrection, which in the Ministration of the Word, is preached or held forth to the hearing of our Ears, so that

[5] "The Baptist Catechism," Question 93, in *The Baptist Confession and the Baptist Catechism* (Birmingham: Solid Ground, 2010), 116.

> we might the better and more effectually be established and grounded in the sure and steadfast belief thereof.[6]

Keach echoes a standard view of the sacraments going back to the early church fathers, namely, the sacraments as visible words. Through these "fit and proper mediums" God preaches to all of our senses a message that "more effectually" establishes and grounds our belief in the gospel. The sacraments strengthen and confirm our faith. Keach appeals not only to the supreme authority of Scripture but also to the testimony of historic Christian authors. The early Baptists dissented from the tradition as regards the subjects of baptism, but they did not see themselves as crafting an utterly novel understanding of the meaning of baptism. Elsewhere, Keach even speaks of baptism as the "Laver of Regeneration," not because it effectively causes regeneration but because it is a "Sign or Figure of it to the Person Baptized."[7]

Thus, the early Baptist view of baptism offers a kind of third way between a merely symbolic understanding of the sacrament ("nothing to see here; this is just a bare sign") and the regenerative understanding of baptism one finds in Roman Catholicism, Eastern Orthodoxy, and some Protestant traditions (such as Lutheranism). Baptism is not the cause of our regeneration, but it is the sign and seal of that regeneration to the new believer. The sacraments are not means of justifying grace; faith alone is the instrument that unites sinners to the justifying obedience of Christ. Instead, the sacraments are means of sanctifying grace, tools that God uses to draw his

---

[6] Benjamin Keach, *Gold Refin'd, or, Baptism in Its Primitive Purity* (London: Nathaniel Crouch, 1689), chapter 4. The full text of this work can be accessed here: https://quod.lib.umich.edu/e/eebo/A47535.0001.001?view=toc

[7] Keach, *Gold Refin'd*, chapter 8.

people, already justified by faith, into closer union with him and to transform them further into Christ's image by his Spirit.

One way we see this in Scripture is through Jesus's command to baptize. Jesus tells his disciples in Matt 28:19, "Go, therefore, and make disciples of all nations, baptizing them in the name of the Father and of the Son and of the Holy Spirit." The subjects of baptism are disciples, those who respond with repentance and faith to the gospel proclaimed by the church. Baptism is "in (or into) the name" of the triune God. In the Bible, the name of God is closely identified with his nature and his presence. Thus, in addition to signifying salvation by God and allegiance to God, baptism also symbolizes the presence of the triune God with all those who trust in him by faith in his crucified and risen Son.

Baptism also signifies the movement from death to life, as Paul notes in Rom 6:3–4 (ESV):

> Do you not know that all of us who have been baptized into Christ Jesus were baptized into his death? We were buried therefore with him by baptism into death, in order that, just as Christ was raised from the dead by the glory of the Father, we too might walk in newness of life.

The immersion of believers into the waters of baptism and the subsequent rise out of those same waters visibly depicts the inner heart change that has occurred through their repentance from sin and their faith in Christ's saving death and resurrection. The Holy Spirit has replaced their hearts of stone with a heart of flesh, and they have thus moved from spiritual death to eternal life in Christ. Baptism is a picture, a symbol, of the gospel. In this way, and when accompanied by the proclamation of the Word, baptism is also a visible proclamation of the gospel and is used by the Spirit to encourage believers and convict unbelievers. This text (along with the New Testament pattern, the meaning of the term *baptizō*, and the practice of the ancient church) undergirds the Baptist insistence upon full immersion as the most faithful mode of baptism. Only immersion fully communicates our complete entrance into death with Christ and our miraculous rescue from death in the resurrection of Christ.

Another way that baptism symbolically proclaims the reality and benefits of the gospel is through its status and use as the sign of the new covenant. Paul speaks of baptism as the new covenant sign (e.g., Col 2:11–12) and as the symbol of the unity that believers have with one another in Christ by the Spirit. Perhaps the most obvious instance of the latter is Eph 4:4–6 (ESV): "There is one body and one Spirit—just as you were called to the one hope that belongs to your call—one Lord, one faith, one baptism, one God and Father of all, who is over all and through all and in all."

In his exhortation to believers to treat one another in a way that demonstrates their unity with one another (Eph 4:1–4 ESV), Paul reminds them of the source of their unity, namely, the Spirit of the Father who has united them to Christ by faith. But notice that Paul here includes not merely the inward, spiritual unity possessed by believers at salvation through their common union with Christ but also their outward unity in the body of Christ as symbolized by "one baptism." Just as, in the old covenant, "our ancestors were all under the cloud, and all passed through the sea, and all were baptized into Moses in the cloud and in the sea" (1 Cor 10:1–2 ESV), so now we all are baptized into Christ in the waters of baptism. The inward reality, inclusion in the new covenant people of God through union with Christ, is symbolized and proclaimed through our common outward sign, water baptism.

All of this symbolism is rooted in the Old Testament and ultimately in the power of our Creator God to use elements of his creation as a way to figure truth about reality. In the Old Testament, we see him use water to signify the movement from chaos or death to order or life and from outside his presence to inside it. We also see water used, many times in concert with the former symbols, as a symbol of entry into God's presence. For instance, the waters of chaos in Gen 1:2 are subdued and parted through God's creative work, and then his image bearers are placed on dry land. In the flood, water is the means of God's judgment, and Noah passes through those waters through God's provision of the ark. After the waters recede, Noah is placed on dry land in God's presence. In the exodus, Israel walks on dry land through the parted waters of the Red Sea, and afterward, those same waters are used to destroy God's enemies, the Egyptian armies. Israel also crosses the Jordan in a similar fashion during their entry into the Promised Land. Finally, Jesus is baptized in the wilderness and, coming out of the water, enters back into Israel and proclaims the good news that he, God the Son in the flesh, has come to defeat the last enemies, sin and death, and give new life to those who follow him. In this way, the baptism of believers in the new covenant is a sign of the renewal of the covenant people of God, of God's victory over our enemies, and of our rescue from death and the gift of eternal life in Christ.

Baptism is a powerful, visible proclamation of the gospel. It signifies the sinner's movement from death to life, from being God's enemy to being perpetually in his presence through the power of the Spirit, and into a union with the covenant people of God. It is not the instrument of justification; faith alone is. Baptism does symbolize all of the blessings of redemption, and it is their covenant sign and seal. When accompanied by the proclamation of the Spirit-inspired Word, it is used by the Spirit as a means of sanctifying grace. It is for this reason the early Baptists felt it appropriate to refer to it, along with the Lord's Supper, as a sacrament.

Baptism as Christ-Commanded Ordinance

Now we can return to the focus of much Baptist writing and thought about baptism in the twentieth and twenty-first centuries—baptism as an ordinance. While early Baptists were comfortable using the terms *sacrament* and *ordinance* interchangeably, there has been a noticeable preference for the latter since at least the late nineteenth century. Baptism is certainly commanded by Christ (Matt 28:19), and it is fitting to refer to baptism as an ordinance, one among several others, including the Word, the Lord's Supper, and prayer. Baptism is the first step of obedience in the Christian life, as the new believer follows Christ's commands. However, we should also urge our fellow Baptists to refrain from treating baptism as merely an ordinance, as if baptism is simply a perfunctory duty we must perform in order to be in compliance with Christ's arbitrary codes of conduct. Jesus had a very clear reason for commanding baptism—because it is a powerful symbol of the truths and benefits of the gospel, and it is also used by the Spirit, when accompanied by the Word, to proclaim that gospel to believers and unbelievers.

Conclusion

It is an encouragement to believers to remember their baptism and recall who they are in Christ. Baptism is a call to the unbeliever, that unless they repent and believe, they will face the waters of judgment without the mercy of Christ. Baptism is discipleship and evangelism. It is sign, sacrament, and ordinance. Baptists of all people should, therefore, take it seriously and teach our people about its significance at every opportunity.

CHAPTER 7

A Believers' Congregational Church

As with believers' baptism, congregational governance is what follows from the Baptist commitment to liberty of conscience. The two commitments of liberty of conscience followed by believers' baptism actually pave the way for the Baptist commitment to a believers' congregational church. The logic for a believers' church is simple. The new covenant people of God includes those who are united to Christ in faith (liberty of conscience), and only those included in the new covenant people of God should receive the new covenant sign of baptism (believers' baptism). Therefore, the church, the new covenant people of God, only consists of those who are united to Christ in faith and have received the sign of the new covenant (a believers' church).

The second affirmation of Baptist ecclesiology (the doctrine of the church) is that this believers' church is also congregational. The logic for this commitment also flows from liberty of conscience corporately, rather than purely individually. The commitment to congregationalism arises out of the fact that Christ is King not only over individual consciences but also over individual churches.

A Believers' Church

Baptists affirm that the new covenant people of God, the church, is made up of those who have responded to Christ in faith and received the new covenant sign of baptism. This affirmation distinguishes Baptists from other Christian traditions that affirm a "mixed body" (*corpus permixtum*).[1] According to these traditions, the church includes both believers and unbelievers in that not all those who are baptized as infants grow up to affirm the faith of their parents. It is not up to the church but to God alone to sort between "the wheat and the tares," so this understanding goes. God will make these distinctions plain as the church rightly preaches the gospel and administers the sacraments and ultimately at the judgment seat of Christ.

In contrast to this understanding, Baptists believe that the church has a responsibility to baptize only those who give a credible profession of faith. This necessarily means that infant baptism is not practiced or even affirmed as baptism. But it also means that the nature of the church, and each individual church, is "regenerate." The church's membership consists of only those who have given a credible profession of faith and received the sign of the new covenant, baptism. Membership in each individual church assumes that each member is regenerate, saved by grace alone through faith alone in Christ alone to the glory of God alone, and thus made new by the Holy Spirit of God.

Some object to this idea of "regenerate church membership" by arguing that God alone knows ultimately and truly who is and is not regenerate. There are those who are baptized into the faith and into church membership at Baptist churches and others who later reject the faith. To this, Baptists agree. There are those who profess

---

[1] See Augustine, *City of God*, 17.9 and 18.49.

Christ and who are baptized into his name who then fall away, and only God can truly judge each heart. That is why Baptists have also traditionally affirmed a strong notion of church discipline in concert with believers' baptism and covenantal Communion (discussed in the next chapter). For Baptists, church discipline is one of the primary means to ensure the church's membership is actually regenerate, by the Spirit's help and to the best of their ability. Those who are repeatedly confronted, exhorted, and rebuked about their patterns of sinful behavior are eventually removed from the church's membership and treated as unbelievers until they repent and return to the church and thus give evidence of their status as believers.

This emphasis on a regenerate church is also an emphasis on the Spirit's role in the church. It is the Spirit who creates the church by uniting believers to the Lord Jesus and to one another through the act of an individual's faith. It is the Spirit who guides, leads, and directs the church through his presence in the preaching of the Word and the administration of the sacraments. Ultimately, it is the Spirit who indwells each individual believer at regeneration, making it possible for that person to be led corporately by him. Because each individual believer is united to Christ and indwelt by the Spirit, he or she is also united to others by the same Spirit. And because believers are united to Christ and to one another by the Spirit, they are also led by the Spirit through the preaching of his inspired Word and through the administration of the sacraments.

A Congregational Church

A regenerate church is one which is governed by the Spirit, God the Holy Spirit, who proceeds from the Father and the Son in eternity and who is sent by the Father and the Son in the economy of salvation. The Holy Spirit is the Spirit of Christ the King, who sent him after ascending to the right hand of the Father, where he rules and reigns right now over all things. In a broad sense, the Holy Spirit is Christ's presence in the world, specifically in the midst of his people, the church. More particularly, the Spirit is Christ's ruling presence in the midst of his people. Christ is King over the church, and he exercises his kingship through the presence of his Spirit (e.g., Eph 4:1–16).

Christ leads his church by his Spirit through the preaching of the Word and the administration of the sacraments. Both of these means of grace are used by the Spirit to proclaim Christ's law of love and his gospel of peace to the believing members of the church and unbelievers who may be in attendance. Our concern in this chapter is primarily with the former. Through the preaching of his inspired, inerrant Word, Christ by his Spirit exhorts, rebukes, corrects, and teaches believers (2 Tim 3:16–4:5). The Spirit is active in the preaching, the verbal proclamation of the Word, to exhort believers to right belief and behavior and to discipline them away from wrong belief and behavior. The same is true in the right administration of the sacraments. The Spirit is active in the sacraments, the visible proclamation of the Word, to exhort believers to right belief and behavior and to discipline them away from wrong belief and behavior. Christ by his Spirit is working through the verbal and visible proclamations of his Word to transform believers—the church's members—into his image (see 2 Cor 3:17–18; Rom 8:26–31).

This is the last step in the logic of congregational governance, at least with respect to the fact that the believers collectively govern the church rather than some form of hierarchical governance (elder rule, presbytery, synod, bishop, etc.). Because each member is indwelt by the Spirit and is being transformed into the image of Christ by his Spirit through the preaching of the Word and the administration of the sacraments, each member has equal voice in the governance of the church. In Baptist polity, the whole local congregation is the final human authority under Christ, as evidenced by Jesus's and Paul's teachings on church discipline (Matt 18:17; 1 Cor 5:9–13), in which the congregation is the final authority in matters of discipline; Paul's exhortation that the church must judge even the teaching of an angel or an apostle in light of the gospel message (Gal 1:8); and the congregation's ultimate authority in choosing its leaders, both elders and deacons (e.g., Acts 6:1–6 ESV, "the whole gathering").[2] This idea is dependent on Baptist churches following through on their commitments to the right preaching of the Word, the right administration of the sacraments, and the faithful exercise of church discipline. If any of these are not functioning properly, there is a high likelihood that a church is allowing undisciplined members to exercise authority over the church. In a healthy church where these fundamental practices are functioning properly, we can trust one another to seek the Spirit's guidance through his Word and govern the church together by his Spirit.

This is another way of saying that Baptists are committed to liberty of conscience. Within a local church, no one member, including the pastor, exercises governing authority over another. Instead, we all individually and corporately seek the guidance of the Spirit through his Word in decision making. Baptists are committed to the priesthood of all believers. Every believer has equal access to the throne room of God through Christ's blood and by his Spirit. Every believer is indwelt by the Spirit of God. Every believer is being conformed into the image of Christ by his Spirit. Therefore, every

---

[2] For a fuller, historical, and biblical defense of congregationalism, see John Hammett, *Biblical Foundations for Baptist Churches: A Contemporary Ecclesiology* (Nashville: B&H Academic, 2005), 146–48; and the first two chapters in Mark Dever and Jonathan Leeman, ed., *Baptist Foundations: Church Government for an Anti-Institutional Age* (Nashville: B&H Academic, 2015).

believer is called to seek the Spirit's guidance in decision making and to deliberate together with his or her fellow members to submit themselves together to Christ the King by his Spirit and under the guidance of his Word.[3]

This does not mean that Baptist churches do not have leaders. Historically and biblically, Baptists affirm two offices for each local church, elders and deacons. While the term *pastor* is more common these days than *elder*, these two terms are synonymous in the New Testament (along with *overseer* or *bishop*). Deacons lead through service (1 Tim 3:8–13). They are not, in the New Testament, a decision-making body but instead lead through serving the church and the community in which the church resides. In particular, they serve the church through handling tasks that free the pastors to focus on preaching, prayer, and pastoral counsel (Acts 6).

Baptists have historically and biblically viewed the office of elder as reserved for men (e.g., 1 Tim 2:12). While some Baptist churches today have shifted on this issue and now allow female pastors, our perspective, which aligns with the historic teaching of both the catholic and the Baptist tradition, is that the teaching of the New Testament limits the office of elder or pastor to qualified men (1 Tim 3:1–7). These men are called to preach the Word, shepherd the flock of God through prayer and counsel, and serve as an example to those in their care. While there is evidence throughout Baptist history that a plurality of elders is common for Baptist churches, and while this accords with New Testament evidence, Baptists have also seen fit to have only one pastor or elder in a given church. Many times, this is due simply to the lack of other qualified men to serve as pastors for that particular congregation. In either case, pastors are not the final decision makers for the church; that responsibility still falls to

[3] See Hammett, 148–49.

members, with pastors included. Pastors still lead through preaching and prayer and pastoral care, but they are not (nor are deacons) the rulers or governors of their congregation. The congregation itself governs together.[4]

This brings us to the final aspect of Baptists' commitment to a congregational church. Congregationalism entails not only that members of local churches govern together, but also that no other church, group of churches, individual, or set of individuals governs any local church. Each local church governs itself. This reflects the Baptist commitment to liberty of conscience. Just like each individual Christian is responsible for himself or herself, so is each local church. Christ is King over the individual conscience and over the individual church. He exercises authority in both cases in the same way: by his Spirit, through the preaching of the Word and the administration of the sacraments.

Commitment to congregational governance does not mean that each Baptist church operates in isolation from one another. While no church governs another, Baptists have still seen fit to associate with one another for missions and ministry. They see this modeled in the New Testamant, when churches work together to support one another (see Acts 15; Rom 15:24, 28; 1 Cor 16:1–4). Historically, Baptists have attempted to follow this model through associationalism. In particular associations, a group of Baptist churches agrees to cooperate for missions and ministry. They often choose to work together to send missionaries to unreached people at home and around the world, to plant churches in places where gospel witness needs to be bolstered, and to educate those called to ministry for the sake of the churches in that association.

[4] See Hammett, 159–215.

In this agreement to cooperate, Baptist churches also typically commit to hold one another accountable with respect to sound doctrine and right practice. No one church can tell another church what to do, but a group of churches who have chosen to associate can deem that a particular church in that association has drifted in either belief or practice (or both). In that case, the association of churches can vote to rebuke the errant church and remove them from the association. This does not have any impact on the operation of the errant church; they are still autonomously governed by their own members and can continue to operate as they see fit. By disassociating from them, however, the association issues a verdict about the limits of their association and declares that the errant church has unwaveringly crossed a doctrinal or moral line. The goal for this kind of action is faithfulness on the part of the association and also a gospel-fueled rebuke to the errant church in hopes that they might repent and return to faithfulness. This is the corporate version of church discipline.[5]

Conclusion: A Believers' Congregational Church

For these reasons and in this fashion, Baptists are committed to a believers' congregational church. Each local church is governed by its own members, each of whom is indwelt by the Spirit and, in submission to Christ the King, is guided by the same Spirit. While each Baptist church has two offices, pastor or elder and deacon, these officers do not govern the church on their own. Instead, the members together, including those officers, seek Christ's guidance by his Spirit through his Word. No other local church governs them, but they can choose to associate with other local, like-minded churches for the purpose of missions and ministry.

---

[5] See Dever and Leeman, ed., *Baptist Foundations*, 331–81.

CHAPTER 8

Covenantal Communion

The Lord's Supper, the other ordinance recognized by Baptists and other Protestants, is inaugurated and commanded by Christ like baptism. It has been celebrated regularly by Christians throughout space and time. It is referred to not only as the Lord's Supper but also as the *Eucharist*, or *Communion*. Although these latter two words, like *sacrament*, are not necessarily used frequently by Baptists and may have negative connotations due to their connection with Roman Catholicism, Baptists need not be afraid of using them. Early Baptists used these phrases to refer to the Lord's Supper. In this chapter, we will stick with common Baptist language and refer to it mostly as the Lord's Supper or Communion. Still, we would also argue that *Eucharist* is a perfectly valid term, since it is simply an English way to use the Greek term for "thanksgiving." Indeed, this meal is a meal of thanksgiving in which we express gratitude for what Christ has done for us in his substitutionary death and resurrection. What else it means and how it is practiced distinctively by Baptists is the subject of this chapter.

The Significance of the Supper

We should begin by reviewing the biblical language about the Supper to establish and emphasize what the Bible says about Communion so that we can properly understand its theological and ecclesiological (churchly) significance. Only when we know what the Supper is can we say how it ought to be conducted.

Israel's Restoration[1]

First, the Lord's Supper is inaugurated by Jesus as a sign of Israel's restoration in himself. The fundamental sign of salvation for Israel in the Old Testament is the exodus event when the Lord delivers Israel from bondage in Egypt through a series of signs that culminate in the death of the firstborn son. Israel is saved from this final judgment by covering their doors with the blood of the lamb from what is later called the Passover meal—prepared and eaten in haste so that Israel could flee immediately from the presence of the judged nation of Egypt. After Israel is brought out from Egypt and taken to Mount Sinai—and, ultimately, to the Promised Land—they are told by God to celebrate this event once a year by eating a commemorative Passover meal. The Passover celebration becomes both a time to look back at what God has already done and an opportunity to look forward to when the Lord will fulfill all his promises made to Abraham and Israel. This forward-looking aspect of the meal becomes increasingly prominent after Israel splits into two kingdoms that both are eventually exiled by the end of 2 Kings. The prophets use the Passover to look forward to God's restoration of Israel through a new exodus, inaugurated with a new Passover meal. For instance, at the end of Hosea, God promises to restore Israel, and he declares his redemptive purposes using the earthy symbols of grain and vine:

---

[1] The material in the section titled "Israel's Restoration" is adapted from Matthew Y. Emerson, "Earthy Signs of Israel's Restoration," *Biblical Reasoning,* February 28, 2017. https://secundumscripturas.com/2017/02/28/earthy-signs-of-israels-restoration/.

They shall return and dwell beneath my shadow;
    they shall flourish like the grain;
they shall blossom like the vine;
    their fame shall be like the wine of Lebanon.
(Hos 14:7 ESV)

Joel reverses this earthy restoration with a promise of the Lord's judgment:

The fields are destroyed,
    the ground mourns,
because the grain is destroyed,
    the wine dries up,
    the oil languishes.
(Joel 1:10)

Notice that a third earthy element, oil, is added into the mix. We could also add here the sign of water; throughout the Old Testament, water is a sign of judgment in both its excess (e.g., Genesis 6) and its lack, as well as a sign of restoration (e.g., Ezek 47:1–12). For Israel, the earthy signs that they are looking for, the signs that demonstrate that the Lord has renewed them through his Messiah and Spirit, are water, oil, grain, and vine (see Deut 7:13 for the initial promise of blessing via these elements). Israel's redemption is pictured as a redemption of the land, and particularly of those four elements.

Jesus came as Israel's "Messiah" or "anointed One." He was anointed both at the beginning of his ministry in baptism and with oil at the end of his ministry, just before his passion (Matt 26:6–13). Jesus embodied these restorative signs of Israel's salvation, water and oil, in his Messianic anointing. With respect to the grain and vine, two elements crucial to Israel's commemorative and formative

Passover meal, Jesus embodied these as well, this time in the Last Supper. As he broke the bread and took the cup, identifying them as his body and blood, he took up the rich symbolism of Israel's redemptive hope and culminated it in himself. There is now bread to eat, and there is now the fruit of the vine to drink in Christ. We could also point to the "I AM" statements in John; Jesus is Israel's bread, light (associated with oil lamps), living water, and vine.

Jesus took all these earthy symbols of Israel's redemptive hope upon himself and fulfilled them. He was the fulfillment of all of Israel's hopes, including its hope of restored land. By taking these earthy symbols on himself, Jesus declared that in him Israel, including the land itself, is redeemed. All of Israel's promises, including the land promises, were fulfilled in the incarnate Son.

But neither Jesus nor the New Testament stop there with respect to these symbols. These earthy symbols were not only fulfilled in Jesus but also instituted as signs of his kingdom. Jesus is Israel's Messiah and King, but he does not isolate the presence of the kingdom in his person. Through pouring out his Spirit at Pentecost, Jesus spread his kingdom from Jerusalem to the ends of the earth via the proclamation of the gospel by his church. As his Spirit-filled church expands, they bring with them signs of the kingdom—the Lord's Supper and baptism. These two ordinances are instituted by Christ as signs of the kingdom because they are signs of Israel's redemption in him and Israel's restoration as God's people in Christ's multiethnic church.

Jesus's body and blood—Israel's redeemed grain and vine—are proclaimed to us in the Supper; therefore, the Supper is a sign of Israel's redemption. Jesus's death and resurrection are proclaimed to us in baptism; therefore, our identification with Christ in our submergence into and reemergence out of the waters is a sign of Israel's redemption. As we anoint ministers, we anoint them (historically with oil) to minister the Word—the vehicle of Christ's authority in his Church—to his people. The congregation sits under the kingship of the anointed Christ as anointed ministers proclaim his Scriptures. The church's symbols are Israel's symbols. Thus, as the church worships Christ, they are doing so as the renewed and restored Israel, the Israel of God, because they are united to Israel's Messiah who redeemed Israel in his own flesh.

Corporate Communion[2]

The Lord's Supper, celebrated weekly in some traditions, is the culmination of what has been sung, prayed, read, and preached thus far in corporate worship. At the Table, we remember the sacrifice that Christ offered on our behalf once and for all. Christ is spiritually present with his people, strengthening and confirming their faith.[3] Christ's people also renew their communion with one another; confession is made, and forgiveness is visually and bodily proclaimed and received. As Paul says in 1 Cor 10:16–17, by partaking in the bread and cup, we are fellowshipping with Christ's body and blood and with one another. This is not an *ex opere operantis* event,[4] nor is it efficacious simply because of the pastor who administers it. Rather, the Lord's Supper is the gospel Word visually and bodily proclaimed, necessarily accompanied by the verbally proclaimed words of institution ("This is my body," etc.). Thus, Word and

---

[2] The section titled "Corporate Communion" is adapted from Matthew Y. Emerson and R. Lucas Stamps, "Liturgy for Low-Church Baptists," *CTR* 14.2 (Spring 2017): 71–88.

[3] This should not be a controversial statement, since all Christians believe (or should believe) God is present in Christ by his Spirit during the gathering of his church for worship.

[4] *Ex opere operantis* means "in virtue of the agent." In other words, by saying that the Lord's Supper is not an *ex opere operantis* event, we are saying that it is not effective by itself just because the person who administers it is certified to do so (i.e., in Roman Catholic theology, an ordained priest).

sacrament belong together. The Lord's Supper is the gospel proclaimed visibly and materially.[5]

We should pause here and make a few clarifications about the Lord's Supper and the way in which we speak of it. First, the language of "sacrament" can be a stumbling block for many Baptists and Low Church evangelicals. In one sense, this reticence is understandable, since the Roman Catholic doctrine of transubstantiation and the Lutheran articulation of consubstantiation have introduced confusion and error to what happens in the celebration of the Supper.[6] By the term *sacrament*, we mean neither transubstantiation nor consubstantiation, both of which are rooted in Aristotelian misconceptions rather than in the biblical text. We reject any notion of the corporeal (bodily) presence of Christ in the sacramental elements. Further, we deny any sense of automatic sacramental efficacy, in which baptism and the Lord's Supper affect the justification of the sinner or infuse Christ's righteousness to the participant.[7] Instead,

---

[5] This is a statement with which virtually every Christian tradition, including the various Baptist traditions, finds agreement. We could call it the baseline for the meaning of the Supper. See Brian J. Vickers, "Celebrating the Past and Future in the Present," in *The Lord's Supper: Remembering and Proclaiming Christ Until He Comes,* ed. Thomas R. Schreiner and Matthew R. Crawford, in NAC Studies in Bible and Theology (Nashville: B&H Academic, 2010), 313–40, who begins his essay by noting that "Most people would say that the Supper somehow symbolizes Christ's death on the cross, the forgiveness of our sins, and perhaps has something to do with Christ's second coming," 313.

[6] For an introduction to the Roman Catholic view of the Supper, see Gregg R. Allison, "The Theology of the Eucharist according to the Catholic Church," in *The Lord's Supper,* ed. Schreiner and Crawford, 151–92. For an introduction to Martin Luther's view of the Supper, see Matthew R. Crawford, "On Faith, Signs, and Fruits: Martin Luther's Theology of the Lord's Supper," in *The Lord's Supper,* ed. Schreiner and Crawford, 193–228.

[7] For a brief overview of this position, as well as Protestant arguments against it, see Alister E. McGrath, *Christian Theology: An Introduction*, 5th ed. (Oxford: Wiley-Blackwell, 2011).

we mean "sacrament" in its more traditional sense: an outward and visible sign of an inward and invisible grace.[8] Christ's presence is communicated to believers via created means. The efficacy of the sacraments is contingent on the proclamation of the Word and the faith of the participants.[9] In this manner, we can rightly speak of the Lord's Supper as a sacrament—a sign and seal of the grace effected in the lives of believers by the work of Christ.[10] Consider Baptist New Testament scholar Brian Vickers's reflections on Luke 24:

> In the Emmaus Road account, Luke draws attention to the disciples' response to Jesus' teaching—their hearts were burning—and to the revelation of Him in the breaking of bread. As Christ is made known through faith in the preaching of the gospel ("faith comes from hearing and hearing through the word of Christ," Rom 10:17), so Christ is present to us by faith when we take up the sym-

[8] This definition is associated with St. Augustine, but we do not wish to endorse the entirety of his particular sacramentology. The Latin *sacramentum* means something like "sacred oath." The Eastern tradition uses the language of *musterion* (mystery) to speak of the sacraments.

[9] On this definition of *sacrament*, see Michael Horton, *The Christian Faith: A Systematic Theology for Pilgrims on the Way* (Grand Rapids: Zondervan Academic, 2011), 766–69.

[10] This was the prevailing view among Baptists for the first two centuries of their existence. See Michael A. G. Haykin, "'His Soul-Refreshing Presence': The Lord's Supper in Calvinistic Baptist Thought and Experience in the 'Long' Eighteenth Century," in *Baptist Sacramentalism*, ed. Anthony R. Cross and Philip E. Thompson, in Studies in Baptist History and Thought 5 (Eugene, OR: Wipf & Stock, 2003). Although Haykin's chapter focuses on Calvinistic Baptists, this should not be taken to mean that a sacramental view was absent from General Baptist thought. On the contrary, see Articles XXXVI–XXXVIII of the General Baptists' "Orthodox Creed (1678)," in *Baptist Confessions of Faith*, ed. Lumpkin and Leonard, 325–27. See also Fowler, *More than a Symbol*, 298–347.

bols that He Himself described as His body and blood. Though Jesus is not revealed visibly to us in the Supper, He is seen by faith through the analogy of the bread and the cup. Just as the body is sustained by food and drink, so we are made and kept alive by the sacrifice of Christ.[11]

And again:

The symbols may be said to *reveal* Jesus as they serve to remind believers that salvation comes only through His body and blood, and that only those who partake of Him will be saved.[12]

And finally:

The bread and cup contain the story of the gospel, and the Supper is a means of reinforcing that in the lives of believers. Understood in this way, the elements are not incidental or immaterial, much less can they be disposed with—they are tangible reminders that Christ came down to us in flesh and blood and died for our sins to bring us to God. . . . Therefore, the bread and the cup do not create faith or make faith possible; but must be grasped in faith so as to remind us that in Christ we are forgiven, rest in a covenant relationship with God, are made in Christ, freed from bondage to sin, and await the day when we will see the One who died, rose again, and ascended into heaven.[13]

---

[11] Brian J. Vickers, "Celebrating the Past and Future in the Present," in *The Lord's Supper*, ed. Schreiner and Crawford, 334–35, emphasis ours.

[12] Vickers, 335, emphasis original.

[13] Vickers, 336–37.

While we understand that some may be uncomfortable with the term *sacrament*, we remain unconvinced that it should be jettisoned. The abuse or misuse of a term does not necessitate abstinence from its proper use, and we believe *sacrament* can still be defined and used properly.[14] The term communicates that the Supper is not merely a memorial but is also a means by which Christ communicates his presence, or in Vicker's words, "reveals himself," through creaturely means. The confessing and remembering believer is not the only or main actor on the sacramental stage. Christ himself assumes this starring role, with the corporate body and the individual believer cast in supporting roles. In the Lord's Supper, the risen Christ seats us around his Table and girds himself to serve us with his blessed presence as we commune with him in the Spirit.[15]

We also believe that this understanding of *sacrament* is consistent with how the Bible speaks of the Lord's Table. In 1 Corinthians 10, Paul gives a lengthy argument about the relationship between Israel, idol worship, and the Lord's Supper. Paul begins in vv. 1–5 by describing Israel's wilderness meals, noting that the food and drink the Lord gave them in the wilderness was "spiritual," and that they drank from the rock, which was Christ. Israel's nourishing meal in their wilderness wandering was both spiritual and a partaking in Christ himself. Paul goes on to say that, while Israel partook in drinking Christ himself, many of them were idolaters, and for this

---

[14] It is also worth noting that many of the earliest Baptists had no compunction in speaking about the Supper in sacramental terms. See the many helpful essays in Cross and Thompson, ed., *Baptist Sacramentalism,* for more historical background.

[15] This "dramatic" rendition of the Supper is inspired by Michael Horton's use of the drama metaphor. See Michael S. Horton, *Covenant and Eschatology: The Divine Drama* (Louisville: Westminster John Knox, 2002). See also Kevin J. Vanoozer, *The Drama of Doctrine: A Canonical Linguistic Approach to Christian Theology* (Louisville: Westminster John Knox, 2005) and the magisterial treatment of the drama metaphor in Hans Urs von Balthasar, *Theo-Drama: Theological Dramatic Theory*, 5 vols. (San Francisco: Ignatius, 1988).

they were judged (vv. 6–13). Paul then compares the church's meal, the Lord's Supper, both to Israel's sacrifices in the tabernacle and to pagan idolaters' sacrifices in their temples. Just as Israel "participates" in the altar (v. 18), and as pagans "participate" with demons, so also Christians "participate" or "fellowship" with Christ's body and blood in the eating of the bread and drinking of the cup in the Supper (v. 16 ESV). Further, not only does the Church fellowship with Christ, but they also fellowship with one another (v. 17 ESV). Because of this participation with Christ at the Table, Christians are warned against idolatry (v. 14), since that would mean that they are fellowshipping with both Christ and demons (vv. 19–22), an unthinkable scenario to Paul.

It is difficult to imagine the exegetical steps required to strip all sacramental notions from the "participation" (*koinōnia*) language of vv. 16–17 ESV. Though the Supper calls us to look back to the cross, this is no mere memorial; Paul is comparing this meal both to Israel's meal in the wilderness and to pagan idol sacrifices. Both of those meals effect union—either with Christ (in the wilderness) or with demons (in pagan idolatry). The church's meal, therefore, is also a participation, a partaking of union with God in Christ, just as Israel's meal was partaking in the presence of God in Christ in the wilderness and just as pagan idolatrous meals are partaking in the presence of demons.[16] For this reason, speaking about the Supper in sacramental terms—not only as a memory of Christ, but also as a real spiritual participation with him—finds warrant in the text of the New Testament itself.[17]

---

[16] For a careful reading of 1 Corinthians 10 that supports the reading here, even while refraining from using the term *sacrament*, see James M. Hamilton, "The Lord's Supper in Paul: An Identity-Forming Proclamation of the Gospel," in *The Lord's Supper,* ed., Schreiner and Crawford, 68–102, especially 73–76.

[17] The view we have defended here can be considered a version of the so-called spiritual presence view associated with John Calvin and the Reformed tradition

The Supper is a particular "means of grace," a term used by early Baptists to describe both preaching and the ordinances.[18] These central elements of corporate worship are God-ordained means of conveying his presence and of transforming his people by his Spirit. The Spirit transforms God's people when they behold Christ (2 Cor 3:17–18), and the preaching of the Word and its visual proclamation in the ordinances are the particular ways God has ordained that they see Jesus. The early Baptists spoke about the Lord's Supper in ways that were consistent with their fellow reformational brethren. Consider the statement on the Supper in the Second London Confession:

> Worthy receivers, outwardly partaking of the visible elements in this ordinance, do then also inwardly by faith, really and indeed, yet not carnally and corporally, but spiritually receive, and feed upon Christ crucified, and all the benefits of his death; the body and blood of Christ being then not corporally or carnally, but spiritually

---

that came in his wake. In this understanding, believers at the Lord's Table have real communion with the whole person of Christ (including his body and blood), but his presence is communicated to them in the meal by the Holy Spirit and is not locally present in the elements of the Lord's Supper. This also appears to be the view of the Supper adopted by many of the earliest Baptists, both Calvinist and non-Calvinist alike.

[18] See Article 14.1 of "The Second London Baptist Confession of Faith," in *Baptist Confessions of Faith,* ed. Lumpkin and Leonard, 261–97, which says, "The Grace of Faith, whereby the Elect are enabled to believe to the saving of their souls, is the work of the Spirit of Christ in their hearts; and is ordinarily wrought by the Ministry of the Word; by which also, and by the administration of Baptisme, and the Lords Supper, Prayer and other Means appointed of God, it is increased, and strengthened." For a contemporary defense of this view, see Richard C. Barcellos, *The Lord's Supper as a Means of Grace: More than a Memory* (Geanies House, UK: Christian Focus, 2013).

> present to the faith of believers in that ordinance, as the elements themselves are to their outward senses.[19]

This perspective has been referred to as the "spiritual presence" view of the Lord's Supper, which has its roots in the continental Reformed tradition. The General Baptists' Orthodox Creed echoes the same kind of language. The risen Lord Jesus Christ is really and truly present to the faithful when they partake "worthily" in the meal. He is not carnally or corporally (that is, bodily) present in the elements. This is not transubstantiation nor consubstantiation, but neither is it a bare memorialism. The Lord's Supper is a memory; the dominical words, "This do in remembrance of me," are carved into the tables of our sanctuaries. But it is also more than a memory. It is one of the special places that Christ has promised to meet us by the Spirit in order to strengthen and confirm our faith. Early Baptist pastor and theologian Benjamin Keach even referred to the Supper as a "soul-reviving cordial," in which there is a "mystical Conveyance or Communication of all Christ's blessed Merits to our souls through Faith."[20]

We are, therefore, comfortable referring to the Table and baptism not only as ordinances but also as sacraments and means of grace, visual proclamations of Christ that convey his presence, his transforming power through the work of his Spirit, and our communion with one another.[21]

---

[19] "The Second London Confession," Article 30, in *Baptist Confessions of Faith* ed., Lumpkin and Leonard, 292–95.

[20] Cited in Michael A. G. Haykin, "Baptists, the Lord's Supper, and the Christian Tradition," in *Baptists and the Christian Tradition: Towards an Evangelical Baptist Catholicity*, ed. Matthew Y. Emerson, Christopher W. Morgan, and R. Lucas Stamps (Nashville: B&H Academic, 2020), 210.

[21] See Vickers, "Celebrating the Past and Future in the Present," 337.

Once the Word is visually and bodily declared at the Table, the congregation is dismissed with a blessing, usually the Aaronic blessing for Israel. In this blessing, the congregation is blessed "to be a blessing." They are commissioned outward into the world in order to proclaim the gospel they have heard, sung, prayed, and seen. The church gathers in worship in order to then scatter into the world, proclaiming the Christ with whom they have shared fellowship through Word and sacrament.[22] The Lord's Supper is both a means of grace and a call to mission.

Baptist Boundaries for the Banquet

Given the significance of the Supper, how then should it be carried out in a local church? Because it is a meal for those who have entered into the new covenant by faith, Baptists have historically understood Communion to be closely tied to baptism. This is not new in the Christian tradition; within the first century or so of Christianity, church leaders made clear that only those who have been

---

[22] On a personal note, one element that is not as prominent in the traditional liturgy, but that we saw practiced well in our church in California, is a focus on the missionary goal of the church. At Redeemer Baptist Church in Riverside, CA, the congregation takes time out of the service to pray for a specific country, usually via the Voice of the Martyrs calendar. Another liturgical element (that came both by providence and an intentionally missional focus) is that Redeemer regularly sends individuals or teams of missionaries to foreign countries, many times to dangerous ones. This means that we often pray not only for global peoples but also for own people going to those global peoples to share the gospel of Jesus Christ. The traditional liturgies certainly have a place for petition, including mission-oriented ones. The Mission St. Clare app now includes a prayer for mission immediately after the Collect, as well as a global peoples prayer calendar, but this has traditionally been a lacuna in the traditional liturgy. It is therefore one area that Baptists—the people that founded the modern missionary movement—can speak back into the tradition, rather than only receive from it.

baptized should be admitted to the Table (*Didachē* 9).[23] This meal is for those who are part of the new covenant people of God. As we have demonstrated in the previous chapters on Baptist understandings of the covenants, liberty of conscience, and baptism, only those who have consciously and credibly professed faith in the Lord Jesus are eligible to receive baptism. So, only those who are baptized can take the Supper, as has been true throughout Christian history. Unique to Baptists, though, is the insistence that only adults (those able to give credible profession of faith) are able to be baptized and thus participate in the Supper.

Historically, Baptists have held at least two positions on setting boundaries for the Table. One of those is called "closed Communion," and argues that only those baptized (by immersion) within a particular local church or who have been admitted to membership at that local church through transfer of membership from a like-minded church may be admitted to the Table. This is because Communion is closely tied to both baptism and church discipline, the former as the proper entry into the new covenant people of God and the latter to ongoing faithfulness to Christ. In that sense, closed Communion is also closely related to congregational church governance. A church who baptizes and disciplines its members is most ably prepared to admit particular members to the Table of the Lord.

A related but distinct position is called "close Communion." In this model, those who have been baptized (by immersion) as adults (those able to give a credible profession of faith) and who are in good standing with their local church may be admitted to the Table, even if they are not members of the local church at which the Supper is being taken. We placed "by immersion" in parentheses in both this

---

[23] "The Didache," in *The Apostolic Fathers: Greek Texts and English Translations*, ed. and trans., Michael W. Holmes, 3rd ed. (Grand Rapids: Baker Academic, 2007), 357–58.

paragraph and the previous one because some Baptist churches are not as insistent about mode of baptism as long as baptism occurred after a credible profession of faith. In either case, both closed and close Communion insist that those admitted to the Table be baptized. The only difference is that closed Communion adds the requirement that the person admitted must be a member of that local church.

A final position, "open Communion," is also practiced by some Baptist churches. In this model, baptism is not necessarily a requirement for the Table. Or, if it is, paedobaptism is accepted by these churches as sufficient. With respect to the former model, in which any professing Christian may be admitted to the Table even if they have not been baptized, we should emphasize that this goes against the entire grain of the Christian tradition. While we are Baptist enough to insist on the autonomy of each local church, we are also committed to historic orthodoxy and orthopraxy. Regarding the latter version of "open Communion," in which paedobaptism is accepted, we should simply note that this prioritizing of the catholicity, or visible unity, of the church over the Baptist distinctive of believers' baptism is highly irregular. Again, we want to insist on the autonomy of the local church here while also pointing out that this logic is inconsistent.

Conclusion: Covenantal Communion

Communion is the covenantal meal taken by all who have entered into the covenant people of God by faith in Christ's finished work and who have followed Christ in baptism. It is for those united to Christ by his Spirit, as Christ is present with each believer and with the whole body corporately. It is also a meal that the Spirit uses to strengthen the bond between believers, conforming them individually and corporately into the image of Christ.

CHAPTER 9

Religious Liberty

A final commitment of Baptists that follows on our understanding of the relation between the covenants and liberty of conscience, believers' baptism, and local church autonomy is that of religious liberty. With the inauguration of the new covenant, the people of God shift from a geopolitical nation-state, Israel, to a community of faith, those united to Christ, the new Israel. The people of God are thus no longer coterminous with a political state. Instead, the boundary marker for the people of God transcends political boundaries; the church is composed of people from every tribe, tongue, and nation through their union with Christ in faith by the Spirit. It is impossible, therefore, for the church to be identified with any particular nation, or for any particular nation to govern spiritual matters that have been left to the church by Jesus. In Matthew 16, Jesus tells Peter that it is his church that possesses the keys to kingdom, not the state. It is Christ's church against whom the gates of hell will not prevail, not the state.[1] It is Christ's church who exercises discipline, not the state. In this chapter, we will explore these twin commitments of religious liberty: (1) the state cannot govern the conscience, including in matters of faith and worship, because (2) there is no longer any

[1] For an introduction to Baptist political theology throughout our history, see Thomas S. Kidd, Paul D. Miller, and Andrew T. Walker, *Baptist Political Theology* (Nashville: B&H Academic, 2023).

particular nation that is chosen by God to be his covenant people. In the new covenant, the people of God consist of people from every tribe, tongue, and nation. We will explore these in reverse order, since the first follows on the second.

Religious Liberty and the New Covenant

The manner of inclusion in the covenant changes with the coming of Jesus. In the old covenant, a person was included by birth, and the sign of the covenant, circumcision, was given at birth. This meant that those in the covenant were physical descendants of Abraham, Isaac, and Jacob—the nation of Israel—and they were given a physical sign of inclusion—circumcision. Because God's people were a nation-state, his law, which governs the spiritual, ceremonial, social, and moral life, was given to the state to enact and uphold. The government of Israel was responsible not only for the social and moral life of the nation but also for its devotional and liturgical life.

We see this in the Ten Commandments, where the first tablet (commandments one through four) governs the spiritual life of Israel, whereas the second tablet (commandments five through ten) governs the social and moral life of Israel. As the Old Testament story makes abundantly clear, not all Israel truly believed in their covenant King and cosmic Creator, the Lord, and they continually disobeyed. The nation-state of Israel included both believers (for instance, Caleb and Joshua) and unbelievers. Because of this mixed body, the Israelites continually failed as a nation to obey either tablet—they did not worship the Lord alone, and so they did not obey either the spiritual or moral commands of the Law. This led to their eventual exile.

In the new covenant, however, Jesus's life and atoning work change how a person is included in the people of God. As the one truly faithful Israelite, Jesus obeyed God's law completely; fulfilled God's promises to Israel, Abraham, and Adam (2 Cor 1:21; Gen 12:1–3; 3:15); paid the penalty for the sins of Israel and of the world at the cross; descended into death to proclaim his victory to the dead (1 Pet 3:18–20); rose from the dead in victory over death and in order to give new life to his people; and ascended into heaven to rule and reign over all nations at the right hand of the Father. He did all that Adam and Israel were called to do but did not, and he reversed the curse of Adam—death—by fulfilling God's promises to Adam and to Abraham. As one of Abraham's and David's lines, he is an Israelite, and because he is the one, truly faithful Israelite, he stands in David's, Abraham's, and Adam's place. Therefore, he now stands in their place as the new Israel and new Adam, and all who are united to him by faith, both Jew and Gentile, are part of the people of God. Because Jesus is the true Israel, everyone who believes in him is also now part of the new Israel. This is not a replacement of the Israel of the Old Testament but instead a fulfillment of all of God's promises to Abraham and his seed through the one seed of woman and descendant of Abraham and David, Jesus Christ, God the Son in the flesh.

The people of God are no longer identifiable with one nation-state among other geopolitical powers in the world. Instead, the people of God are now the church, made up of both believing Jews and believing Gentiles from every tribe, tongue, and nation. For this reason, God has now given authority to the church, not the state, to govern spiritual matters. As Jesus tells Peter in Matt 16:18–19 (ESV),

> And I tell you, you are Peter, and on this rock I will build my church, and the gates of hell shall not prevail against it. I will give you the keys of the kingdom of heaven, and

> whatever you bind on earth shall be bound in heaven, and whatever you loose on earth shall be loosed in heaven.

For Baptists (and other Protestants), the rock on which the church is built is the gospel of Jesus Christ. The keys of the kingdom have historically been understood to be the right preaching of the Word and the right administration of the sacraments. As the Word of God is proclaimed verbally and visibly in preaching and the ordinances, the church of Jesus Christ binds and looses its members. In baptism, we declare that this person has entered from death to life by faith and is now part of the new covenant people of God by the regenerating power of the Holy Spirit and by their union with Christ. In the Lord's Supper, we declare that each member partaking is united to one another and to Christ and is walking in his grace. In the preaching of the Word, the Holy Spirit convicts us of sin and encourages holiness, prompting discipline among the church's members. The spiritual governance of the people of God is given to the church, not to any particular nation-state, not even to one that is mostly "Christian."

This does not mean that Baptists believe that faith should not influence their nations' governments. Baptists have a long history of using their voice to encourage their governments to act justly and in accordance with God's moral order, stretching back to their origins in seventeenth-century England. The distinction on which they insist is simply that while the state can and should govern the moral and social life of a nation in accordance with the triune God's moral order, the state cannot and is not authorized to govern the spiritual or liturgical life of its citizens. That responsibility is given to the church alone.

Liberty of Conscience and the State

This brings us to the Baptist insistence on religious liberty. It is not born out of a purely political belief that procedural democracy can produce good government but instead out of an understanding of the relation between the covenants and the purpose of the state in light of the first coming of Christ and his inauguration of the new covenant. Because the state cannot and should not govern the spiritual and liturgical life of its citizens, Baptists insist that each person is accountable to God alone with respect to his or her religious beliefs and practices. Each person, and groups of people, should be allowed to worship as they will, so long as they are not bringing harm to others. By "harm," we mean simply some kind of physical violence or aggression, not that any given person's religious beliefs and practices might offend someone else's sensibilities.

While this fundamental commitment of Baptist political theology is rooted in Scripture and our attendant theological commitments, it did not arise in an historical vacuum. Baptist political theology was formed and shaped during periods of political persecution by fellow Christians, both Roman Catholic and Protestant, and in both England and the American colonies. In the chapter on liberty of conscience, we already briefly explored the story of Thomas Helwys, as well as the theology expressed by other British Baptists later in the seventeenth century. Here, we want to also mention Roger Williams, an influential American colonist who had profound impacts on both Baptist and broader political thought regarding religious liberty.

Many who have read even cursory accounts of American history are familiar with Williams, the founder of the Rhode Island colony and, for some, the "father of religious liberty" in the American colonies.[2] Williams first came to the Bay Colony (now Massachusetts) in 1631. During his voyage to the American colonies, he became convinced of Separatism (the idea that the Puritans should separate from the Church of England because of the latter's corruption). While living in the Bay Colony, he clashed with authorities over a number of religious matters, most importantly his convictions regarding religious liberty. This led to his exile from the Bay Colony in 1635 and his establishment of a new colony, eventually chartered by Charles I in 1644 and called Rhode Island.

In Rhode Island, Williams became convinced of credobaptism. In late 1638 or early 1639, another believer baptized Williams, who then baptized that man and ten believers. This is considered to be the founding of the First Baptist Church of Providence, which was also the first Baptist church in America. During Williams's life in Rhode Island, he continued to push for religious liberty and for a charter for this new territory. Regarding the former, he wrote a number of works regarding what he called "soul freedom," including, most importantly, "The Bloudy Tenent of Persecution, for Cause of Conscience" (1644).[3] In this text, Williams makes important and foundational arguments for religious liberty from Baptist principles. Williams famously concludes, based on Baptist theology and hermeneutics, that

> God's people since the coming of the King of Israel, the Lord Jesus, have openly and constantly professed that no civil magistrate, no king nor Caesar, has any power over the souls or consciences of their subjects in the matters

[2] For the summary of Williams that follows, see Chute, Finn, and Haykin, *The Baptist Story*, 28–31.

[3] See James Calvin Davis, ed., *On Religious Liberty: Selections from the Works of Roger Williams* (Cambridge: Belknap Press, 2008), 85–156.

> of God and the crown of Jesus, but the civil magistrates themselves, yea kings and kaisers, are bound to subject their own souls to the ministry and church, the power and government of this Lord Jesus, the King of kings.[4]

For Williams and other early Baptists, in both Britain and the American colonies, the government should not hold the sword of the conscience; that sword is wielded only by Christ through his Spirit and communicated in his Word.[5] Civil governments possess merely the sword of the civil law, which governs outward action but not matters of the heart, including matters of worship and belief.

What Williams and others recognized based on Baptist theology and hermeneutics is that the government cannot and should not tell us what to believe or how to practice our religion. Under the new covenant, authority to govern those kinds of matters is given to the church alone. Each person is responsible to God alone for what he or she believes and how he or she worships. Those who enter into the new covenant by faith are subject to discipline by the church, not the state, because God has given authority to the church to discipline her members in those matters. All citizens of a given nation are thus responsible to God alone for their faith and the exercise of it.

---

4 Davis, 100.

5 Much is often made of Williams's departure from FBC Providence shortly after its founding, as if that is a reason to reject any and all of his conclusions. The reality is, much like John Smyth in England, Williams articulated Baptist beliefs in accordance with a Baptist hermeneutic, even if at a later time he departed from some of those same distinctives. And, others besides both Smyth and Williams continued to articulate Baptist distinctives, including religious liberty, after their respective departures. Helwys held the line after Smyth, and John Clarke and Obadiah Holmes in the American colonies continued to hold and teach Baptist distinctives even after Williams became an isolated schismatic. On the latter, see Chute, Finn, and Haykin, *The Baptist Story*, 31–34.

This does not mean that Christians should not seek to influence the state. God has ordered government to punish evil, which requires a particular nation to be able to tell the difference between good and evil. As Paul notes in Rom 13:1–7 (ESV),

> Let every person be subject to the governing authorities. For there is no authority except from God, and those that exist have been instituted by God. Therefore whoever resists the authorities resists what God has appointed, and those who resist will incur judgment. For rulers are not a terror to good conduct, but to bad. Would you have no fear of the one who is in authority? Then do what is good, and you will receive his approval, for he is God's servant for your good. But if you do wrong, be afraid, for he does not bear the sword in vain. For he is the servant of God, an avenger who carries out God's wrath on the wrongdoer. Therefore one must be in subjection, not only to avoid God's wrath but also for the sake of conscience. For because of this you also pay taxes, for the authorities are ministers of God, attending to this very thing. Pay to all what is owed to them: taxes to whom taxes are owed, revenue to whom revenue is owed, respect to whom respect is owed, honor to whom honor is owed.

As Christians seek to obey God's command to be subject to their government, they are also, as Christ's ambassadors, called to be a prophetic voice to governments, calling them to repent of evil and acknowledge the good. And, they are called to do so according to God's standards, not the world's.

Conclusion

Article 17 of the Baptist Faith and Message 2000 provides a helpful summary of what we have covered in this chapter:

> God alone is Lord of the conscience, and He has left it free from the doctrines and commandments of men which are contrary to His Word or not contained in it. Church and state should be separate. The state owes to every church protection and full freedom in the pursuit of its spiritual ends. In providing for such freedom no ecclesiastical group or denomination should be favored by the state more than others. Civil government being ordained of God, it is the duty of Christians to render loyal obedience thereto in all things not contrary to the revealed will of God. The church should not resort to the civil power to carry on its work. The gospel of Christ contemplates spiritual means alone for the pursuit of its ends. The state has no right to impose penalties for religious opinions of any kind. The state has no right to impose taxes for the support of any form of religion. A free church in a free state is the Christian ideal, and this implies the right of free and unhindered access to God on the part of all men, and the right to form and propagate opinions in the sphere of religion without interference by the civil power.
> Genesis 1:27; 2:7; Matthew 6:6–7,24; 16:26; 22:21; John 8:36; Acts 4:19–20; Romans 6:1–2; 13:1–7; Galatians 5:1,13; Philippians 3:20; 1 Timothy 2:1–2; James 4:12; 1 Peter 2:12–17; 3:11–17; 4:12–19.[6]

---

[6] "XVII: Religious Liberty," *The Baptist Faith and Message* 2000, The Southern Baptist Convention, https://bfm.sbc.net/bfm2000/#xvii.

In light of our political theology, Baptists have early and often exercised this role as sociopolitical prophetic witnesses, calling on their societies and their governments to pursue good and turn from evil. But Baptists have also been among the first to acknowledge that only the gospel can bring truly lasting change. What is needed is not a Christian prince who uses the government's sword to prosecute public displays of unbelief but a church full of Christ's ambassadors who proclaim the gospel to their neighbors from every tribe, tongue, and nation, praying for the Spirit of God to change their hearts and bring them to the Father through faith in his Son, Jesus Christ, our Lord.

PART III

PRACTICES

CHAPTER 10

Worship

Introduction

We have so far explored the theological foundations of the Baptist vision and the ecclesiological distinctives that mark the Baptist way of being the church. At its foundations, Baptist theology is catholic, reformational, and evangelical. Baptists hold to orthodox trinitarianism and Christology, embrace the principles of Reformation soteriology, and express their faith in distinctively evangelical ways. Further, Baptists employ a particular covenantal hermeneutic, reading the Scriptures as a progressive revelation that culminates in the new covenant fulfillment of old covenant promises. This way of reading the Scriptures issues forth in a distinctive ecclesiology, with implications for Baptist polity, piety, and social theory. A commitment to liberty of conscience undergirds the Baptist vision for a believers' church, believers-only baptism, congregationalism, covenantal Communion, religious freedom, and the separation of church and state.

In the final three chapters of this book, we turn our attention more specifically to Baptist practices—the spirituality produced by these theological foundations and ecclesiological distinctives. What does the Baptist vision look like on the ground? We focus attention specifically on three essential Baptist practices: worship, holiness, and mission. In this chapter, we will explore our worship of the triune God, the central feature of Baptist practice.

Pure Worship

In an important work on the origins of the Baptist movement, Baptist historian and worship pastor Matthew Ward states that the quest for pure worship regulated by the Scriptures is not merely one Baptist distinctive among others but the distinguishing mark of the Baptist vision. He suggests that, for the early Baptists, "their hermeneutic, their ecclesiology, and their soteriology" were all "driven by their fundamental desire to worship God purely."[1] According to Ward, the key is an understanding of worship that includes all of the acts of obedience directed immediately toward God by believers, including both external worship (with its ceremonies and ordinances) and internal worship (both private and family worship). Baptists carried the English Separatist principles of worship to their logical conclusions. Worship should be free (not determined by the strictures of the established church), true (regulated by Scripture alone), and gospel-oriented (focused on Christ and his saving acts). This philosophy of worship led the early Baptists to pare down their liturgical ceremonies and to focus only on those elements of worship explicitly laid down in the New Testament. Regardless of how one evaluates Ward's bold thesis, it is difficult to overlook just how important worship was for the development of early Baptist faith and practice.

One of the key debates among Protestants regarding public worship concerns the elements included. According to the *normative principle* of worship, what Scripture does not forbid, it permits.

[1] Matthew W. Ward, *Pure Worship: The Early English Baptist Distinctive* (Eugene, OR: Pickwick 2014), xii.

This approach was characteristic of the established church of England during the post-Reformation period. The normative principle made room for officially sanctioned forms of worship, including the required use of the Book of Common Prayer and the observation of the liturgical calendar, among other ceremonies. However, the *regulative principle* of worship argues that what Scripture does not prescribe, it does not permit. This approach was embraced by the English Puritans and Separatists. Only those elements of worship that are explicitly taught by precept or example in the New Testament are to be included in worship: the reading and preaching of Scripture; prayer; the singing of psalms, hymns and spiritual songs; the observation of baptism and the Lord's Supper; and the collection of offerings.

Emerging as they did from English Separatism, early Baptists tended to embrace this latter, regulative principle of worship. At times, Baptists defended the strictest form of the principle, even disallowing the musical accompaniment in worship, since musical instruments are only mentioned in the Old Testament and not in any New Testament expression of worship.[2] Early Baptists also eschewed the use of images in worship and avoided ornate architecture and furnishings for their "meeting houses." Some also rejected the use of the traditional liturgical calendar, even the celebration of Christmas and Easter, arguing that the only holy days of the new covenant are the fifty-two Sundays of each year. Over time, however, Baptists have loosened their hold on the regulative principle, without fully abandoning it. The regulative principle itself makes a distinction between the elements of worship (the practices determined by God's Word) and the circumstances of worship (the

[2] See Andrew Fuller, *On Instrumental Music in Church Worship*, in Andrew Fuller, *The Complete Works of Andrew Fuller*, 3 vols. (London: Bohn, 1859), 3: 859–61.

time, place, sermon schedule, and so on, which are determined by prudence).[3] While the Reformers and Puritans may have held to a stricter application of this distinction, the regulative principle at least provides a way for Baptists to distinguish what is demanded by Scripture from what may be permitted as an aid to observing those demands. The element of singing, for example, is prescribed by the New Testament, but the use of instruments or electronic amplification is not. However, the latter may be prudentially employed as an aid to practicing the former.

The principle of free worship also gives support to a somewhat looser application of the regulative principle. While set forms of prayer or the commemoration of certain holy days might not be prescribed in the New Testament, they may nevertheless be freely employed by congregations seeking to order their public worship to the Word of God. Since the twentieth century, British Baptists have tended to make more liberal use of the forms of other traditions, including the structure of historic liturgies, the use of prayer books, and the observation of the church year. In more recent decades, Baptists in North America have also followed suit, sometimes giving sustained attention to seasons of the year such as Advent and Lent. These practices need not be seen as a denial of the regulative principle so much as an aid to following it in a theologically comprehensive and historically rooted way. Baptists may disagree about the prudence of such additions, but one of the hallmarks of the Baptist movement is freedom. Congregations are free to use (or not to use) whatever forms and circumstances they deem prudent for the faithful observation of the biblical elements.

---

[3] See Zacharias Ursinus, *The Commentary of Zacharias Ursinus on the Heidelberg Catechism*, trans. G. W. Willard (Cincinnati: Elm Street, 1888), 521.

A Baptist Liturgy?

For many, the juxtaposition of *Baptist* with *liturgy* might sound like an oxymoron. Many associate liturgical worship with the "high church" expressions of Catholicism, Orthodoxy, and Anglicanism. But liturgy is not optional.[4] As many worship historians and practitioners have attested, every church has a liturgy.[5] Every church has some order, structure, and rationale for their "public service" (Greek, *leitourgia*, literally, "the work of the people"). Habits of worship inevitably cement themselves in even the most doggedly extemporaneous services. Routines form, rituals take over, and traditions develop in even the lowest of low churches. So the question is never *whether* liturgy, but always *whither* liturgy—not, Will we worship liturgically?, but How will we worship liturgically and to what end? Will our worship practices be formed according to the Scriptures and in light of the Christian tradition? Or will our worship practices be haphazard, unreflective, and thus ill-suited for the kind of spiritual formation necessary in order to build up the body of Christ?

It is often assumed, both inside and outside the Baptist movement, that Baptists are among the most liturgically impoverished communities of Christian worship. Our services are "low church," we are told. Baptist services tend to be more informal, our worship

---

[4] Portions of this section first appeared in Matthew Y. Emerson and R. Lucas Stamps, "Liturgy for Low-Church Baptists," *Criswell Theological Review* 14, no. 2 (Spring 2017), 71–88.

[5] Robert E. Webber and Rodney Clapp, *People of the Truth: The Power of the Worshipping Community in the Modern World* (Eugene, OR: Wipf & Stock, 1988), 91. See also Mike Cosper, *Rhythms of Grace: How the Church's Worship Tells the Story of the Gospel* (Wheaton: Crossway, 2013), 117; D. G. Hart, *Recovering Mother Kirk: The Case for Liturgy in the Reformed Tradition* (Eugene, OR: Wipf & Stock, 2003), 70.

spaces less ornate, and our rituals less connected to the Christian past. But the relative "height" of our worship need not be limited by the accouterments of services or lack thereof. If our goal is to worship the triune God "in spirit and in truth" (John 4:23–24) "with reverence and awe" (Heb 12:28), then Baptists can ascend the holy mountain of divine worship to peaks just as "high" as our more traditional counterparts, though undoubtedly by different paths.

Contemporary Baptist worship has been shaped by what historian of Christian worship James F. White has called "the frontier liturgy."[6] Forged in the camp meetings and revivals of the Second Great Awakening, this approach to worship focused primarily on the conversion of sinners, not so much on the public worship of God by the already converted. As White explains, these frontier liturgies dramatically reshaped the worship practices of the churches influenced by the revivals. The pattern that emerged from the revivals "still forms the outline of most Protestant worship in North America."[7]

According to White, services influenced by the frontier tradition had three primary parts:

> The first part is a service of prayer and praise which includes considerable musical elements. Congregational singing developed and choirs were introduced. Extempore prayer was offered. And a lesson was read, usually a single lesson, as the basis for the sermon. The second part was fervent preaching, which was the major event of the service (and for which all else sometimes seemed preparatory). The sermon called the unconverted to conversion,

[6] James F. White, *A Brief History of Christian Worship* (Nashville: Abingdon, 1993), 159–61.

[7] White, *A Brief History of Christian Worship*, 161.

> sinners to repentance, and the godly to rejoice in their salvation. The third part was a harvest of those converted or those recommitting their lives to Jesus Christ.[8]

This basic outline—music, sermon, and invitation—would have been familiar to anyone attending the typical Southern Baptist church a generation ago, and likely still influences the vast majority of Baptist churches today. In many ways, this outline has much to commend it biblically. Many of these elements are vital to New Testament worship, especially prayer (Acts 1:14; 2:42; 1 Tim 2:1), praise (Col 3:16, Eph 5:19), and preaching (2 Tim 4:2). The public invitation—especially the "altar call" that emerged in the wake of Charles Finney's "new measures"—is more controversial in many ways.[9] Despite the danger of manipulation present in some forms of the altar call, most Baptist churches have retained some kind of public invitation at the end of their services. As long as safeguards are put in place to prevent abuse, there is nothing unbiblical about providing time and space for a public response to the gospel call issued in the preaching of God's Word. It is positively biblical to issue a public gospel invitation (Acts 2:37–39) and to provide an opportunity for public professions of faith, though this profession is most biblically expressed in believers' baptism, rather than merely "walking the aisle." A public invitation may also provide occasion for prayer and encouragement among the members of the church, giving space for the expression of the manifold gifts in the body of Christ (1 Cor 12:4–11).

---

[8] White, *A Brief History of Christian Worship*,1 61.

[9] For a brief history of the altar call, see Douglas A Sweeney and Mark C. Rogers, "Walk the Aisle," *Christianity Today*, October 27, 2008, http://www.christianitytoday.com/history/2008/october/walk-aisle.html.

The frontier liturgy has several other strengths that commend it, particularly from a Baptist point of view. First, the emphasis on musical worship fits well with one of the particular strengths of historic Baptist worship, namely, hymn writing and singing. This emphasis is often and rightly associated with the Wesleyan tradition, but Baptists have also had their share of influential hymn writers and well-known hymns.[10] Second, the focus on preaching is one of the peculiar strengths of Reformation worship of which Baptists are coheirs along with their fellow Protestants. The recovery of the sermon—the clear and relevant exposition of Scripture—as the centerpiece of Christian worship is one of the great boons of the Reformation era.[11] Finally, the frontier liturgy's emphasis on the gospel message and the need for personal conversion fits well with the evangelistic and missionary impulse that has characterized the Baptist movement throughout its four-hundred-year history.[12]

Frontier liturgy has five possible limitations, though these reflections should not obscure our genuine appreciation for the benefits outlined above. First, without careful attention, the frontier liturgy can become untethered from the historic patterns of gospel-shaped worship that we will discuss in the next section. The narrative structure of historic worship—moving from adoration, the confession of

---

[10] See David W. Music and Paul Akers Richardson, *"I Will Sing the Wondrous Story": A History of Baptist Hymnody in North America* (Macon: Mercer University Press, 2008). But interestingly, the centrality of hymn-singing in Baptist churches was not achieved without controversy. On the seventeenth-century hymn-singing debate, see Matthew Ward, *Pure Worship: The Early English Baptist Distinctive* (Eugene, OR: Pickwick, 2013), 193–203.

[11] On the history of preaching and especially the contributions of the Reformation era, see John R. W. Stott, *Between Two Worlds: The Art of Preaching in the Twentieth Century* (Grand Rapids: Eerdmans, 1982), 15–49.

[12] British Baptist theologian Steve Holmes highlights missions as one of the distinctive themes of Baptist theology. Stephen R. Holmes, *Baptist Theology* (London: T&T Clark, 2012), 141–54.

sin, and the assurance of pardon to thanksgiving, petition, instruction, the celebration of the ordinances, and commissioning—is not always immediately apparent in the pared down organization of the frontier liturgy. Second, the frontier tradition can, perhaps inadvertently, become performance-based, with the musical skill and rhetorical abilities of worship leaders and preachers eclipsing the central speaking role of God in more Word-centered liturgies. Ironically, when evangelical worship orients itself primarily toward the performances on the platform, it can revert back to the passivity of the laity characteristic of some medieval worship, when "worship" was focused on what took place behind the priestly veil, rather than in the pews as the people of God speak back to God in response to his Word.

Third, there is a noticeable scarcity of Scripture readings in frontier liturgy. In many Baptist and evangelical churches, it is not uncommon for there to be only one Scripture reading during the entire service, namely, the sermon text read by the preacher. This practice can be contrasted with more traditional liturgies, which often include four Scripture lessons (readings), taken from different parts of the Bible: the Psalter, the rest of the Old Testament, the epistles, and the gospels. This points to another irony, namely, that many evangelical churches, which place a high priority on the inspiration and inerrancy of Holy Scripture, feature far less Scripture than many "higher" traditions, some of which have long ago abandoned belief in the full trustworthiness of the Bible.[13]

Finally, frontier liturgy is often limited by its principal aim, the conversion of sinners to Christ. While our services should always be

---

[13] Robert Webber notes that this emphasis on Scripture reading is part of what drew him to the Episcopal Church. Robert E. Webber, *Evangelicals on the Canterbury Trail: Why Evangelicals Are Attracted to the Liturgical Church* (Waco: Word, 1985), 41.

intelligible to any unbelieving visitors who may attend our services (1 Cor 14:16), the primary aim of Lord's Day worship should be the glorification of the triune God and the edification of the body of Christ. Richly meaningful worship requires initiation and instruction, and it may not be immediately relevant to those who do not share our commitment to the lordship of Christ. Keeping the twin focus of God and his people in view ought to radically reshape and reorient what we prioritize in the worship experience. We long for conversions, but the public worship of God serves a higher and more fundamental purpose: calling the people of God to a life of service in the love of God and neighbor.

We now turn our attention to historic Christian liturgies, which, while not sidelining the strengths of the frontier liturgy, nevertheless may enrich it with more biblically and historically rooted depth.

Historic Christian Liturgies

While Baptists were active participants in and beneficiaries of the Great Awakenings, the Baptist movement predates frontier liturgy by a century or more. Older Baptist liturgies were still relatively pared down in terms of their ceremonies and were characterized by many of the same elements as frontier liturgy (singing and preaching in particular), but they were less focused on evangelistic outreach and more vertically and horizontally directed. Christ was the focus, and the edification of the body was the intended result. The elements of worship were set by the New Testament prescription: the reading of Scripture, public prayer, psalms and hymns, the preaching of Scripture, baptism, and the Lord's Supper. Baptist worship has tended to be more extemporaneous and less formal but not without a sense of orderliness and reverence.

As Christians, Baptists are also the inheritors of an older tradition of historic Christian liturgy, though their indebtedness to that tradition has not always been explicitly acknowledged or thoroughly explored. In the broadest scope, historic liturgy includes several main movements that reenact the drama of the gospel: gathering, listening, communing, and sending. The faithful are called to worship by God's Word, they listen attentively as the Word is read and preached, they commune with God and one another at the Lord's Table, and they are commissioned to serve the world in the love of God.[14]

Bryan Chappell notes that traditional worship is divided into two major segments: the "Liturgy of the Word" and the "Liturgy of the Table" (or, the "Liturgy of the Upper Room").[15] The Liturgy of the Word is typically preceded by several introductory rites: a scriptural call to worship, the confession of sin, the assurance of divine pardon, and songs of praise and thanksgiving (including ancient hymnic formulas such as the *Kyrie Eleison* and the *Gloria Patri*). The Liturgy of the Word proper includes several Scripture readings (from the Psalter, the Old Testament, the New Testament epistles, and culminating with the Gospels), a sermon, the recitation of an ancient creed, and various prayers. The Liturgy of the Table then ensues, including the following elements: the offertory, the Eucharistic prayer, the Lord's Prayer, the breaking of the bread, an invitation to Communion, Communion itself, and prayers after Communion. The service ends with a concluding rite: a benediction and the dismissal.

---

[14] See James K. A. Smith, *You Are What You Love: The Spiritual Power of Habit* (Grand Rapids: Brazos, 2016), 83–110.

[15] Bryan Chapell, *Christ-Centered Worship: Letting the Gospel Shape Our Practice* (Grand Rapids: Baker Academic, 2009), 19.

Typical Baptist worship bears some resemblance to this basic pattern. There is a call to worship, an invocation, various hymns of praise, a pastoral prayer, an offertory prayer and the collection of tithes and offerings, a Scripture reading, an expositional sermon, a hymn of invitation, and a concluding benediction. Some elements may seem missing from the standard Baptist liturgy—namely, confession and assurance, multiple Scripture readings, and weekly Communion. Regarding the last point, there is variation within the Baptist tradition. Many churches practice quarterly Communion (a tradition that goes back to Zwingli's practice during the Reformation). Other churches are beginning to see the benefit of more regular observance of Communion (monthly or even weekly). There is nothing preventing Baptists from observing the Lord's Supper more frequently. Some worry that this change would make the ordinance too routine and thus lose its significance. Interestingly, no one seems bothered by the weekly singing of hymns, a weekly sermon, or the weekly collection of offerings. The worry about routine also begs the question about the benefits of habitual worship practices. We could do worse than having a weekly reminder and confirmation of the Lord's benefits in the multisensory experience of the Lord's Supper.

Regarding the other "missing" elements from the historic Christian liturgy, there is a sense in which Baptists have practiced these same things through different means. Our hymnals contain many songs of contrition over sin and assurance of divine pardon through the death and resurrection of Christ. The traditional Baptist practice of "testimonies," where a fellow believer shares his or her Christian experience with the whole congregation, is another means of being reminded of our sin and of the Lord's mercy. The invitation itself has provided another opportunity for repentance and assurance. Other elements, such as the Lord's Prayer and the recitation of creeds, can be a most welcome addition to Baptist liturgy. Multiple Scripture readings should be right at home for a denomination that self-consciously identifies as a "people of the Book." The *Baptist Hymnal* even includes responsive readings for public worship. In short, we believe that Baptists can retain what is native to their historic patterns of worship (including frontier liturgy) and at the same time incorporate the best practices of historic Christian liturgies. It is not a matter of either/or, but both/and.

Private and Family Worship

For the early Baptists, worship was a comprehensive term that describes all of the believer's acts of devotion immediately directed toward God. This view is in keeping with the New Testament understanding of worship. The Old Testament ceremonies—the priesthood, the sacrificial system, and the tabernacle and temple—were shadows pointing forward to the substance of Christ and his saving work. By extension, the body of Christ fulfills these Old Testament types in lives of repentance, faith, obedience, and love.[16] As the Apostle Paul puts it, believers' "spiritual worship" is the offering of their whole lives as "a living sacrifice, holy and acceptable to God" (Rom 12:1 ESV). True worship is not confined to the external ceremonies of public worship, foundational though they are for the spirituality of the whole church. True worship also includes both personal and familial exercises of devotion, as well as the whole life of Christian obedience. According to the Second London Confession,

> Neither prayer nor any other part of religious worship, is now under the gospel, tied unto, or made more acceptable

[16] See David Peterson, *Engaging with God: A Biblical Theology of Worship* (Downers Grove: InterVarsity, 1992).

> by any place in which it is performed, or towards which it is directed; but God is to be worshipped everywhere in spirit and in truth; as in private families daily, and in secret each one by himself; so more solemnly in the public assemblies, which are not carelessly nor wilfully to be neglected or forsaken, when God by his word or providence calls thereunto.[17]

In his monumental work, *A Body of Practical Divinity*, eighteenth-century Baptist theologian John Gill devotes twenty-five chapters to the nature of Christian worship, which he understands as both external and internal, before he moves on to the specifics of public worship and family and societal obligations. This section of Gill's work is subtitled, "Practical Religion," which is a fair summary of the Baptist view of worship: our whole lives and all of their practices should be directed toward God in worship. Among the many subjects Gill treats in this section are the theological virtues of faith, hope, love, humility, the fear of God, self-denial, and communion with God.

Conclusion

Baptists have typically held to a high view of the Lord's Day, which many have understood as the "Christian Sabbath," though some in recent decades have adopted a non-sabbatarian view of the Lord's Day. Regardless of one's position in that particular debate, all Baptists should mark the day of the Lord's resurrection with exercises of worship both public and private. Christians are obligated to pray daily as both individuals and families so that they can render

---

[17] "The Second London Baptist Confession of Faith," Article 22, in *Baptist Confessions of Faith*, ed., Lumpkin and Leonard, 278.

spiritual worship to the triune God with their whole selves. Nothing should be more important to the Christian than this: giving God the glory that is due his name for his infinite perfections and for all gracious benefits.

CHAPTER 11

Holiness

Introduction

As noted earlier, if we had to pick a "life verse" for the Baptist vision, the Great Commission of Matthew 28:18–20 (ESV) would be a leading candidate:

> And Jesus came and said to them, "All authority in heaven and on earth has been given to me. Go therefore and make disciples of all nations, baptizing them in the name of the Father and of the Son and of the Holy Spirit, teaching them to observe all that I have commanded you. And behold, I am with you always, to the end of the age."

According to Baptist theologian Steve Holmes, this passage highlights two "central Baptist concerns: mission and holiness."[1] Baptists have been especially committed to the task of making disciples of all nations (through both personal evangelism and local and global missions) and then to the task of teaching the converted to observe all the Lord's teachings. In the final two chapters of this book, we will

[1] Stephen R. Holmes, *Baptist Theology* (London: Continuum, 2012), 141.

explore these two interrelated concerns in reverse order: holiness in this chapter and mission in the next.

We might tend to identify holiness with some other Christian tradition, for example, the Wesleyan movement or the Holiness tradition that emerges from it. All Christians are committed to obeying the Lord Jesus in a life of discipleship, so this is not an exclusively Baptist distinctive. But it does have a distinct inflection in Baptist faith and practice, given our commitment to a believers' church as a covenanted community of visible saints who correct, admonish, encourage, and support one another in the pilgrimage of faith. The Baptist vision has its eyes set on Christ and seeks to be conformed together into his image by God's grace.

A Church of Visible Saints

In his ground-breaking 2019 book, *Orthodox Radicals: Baptist Identity in the English Revolution*, Baptist historian Matthew Bingham suggests a reevaluation of our understanding of Baptist origins.[2] His central thesis is that the early "Particular Baptists" have been anachronistically mislabeled "Baptist," as if there was already an existing pan-Baptist movement to which these Separatists could naturally join themselves (including the so-called General Baptists which had emerged earlier in the century). Bingham further suggests that this mislabeling in the historiography of Baptist origins has obscured the theological logic that led many Congregationalists to a rejection of infant baptism. Instead, Bingham argues that the groups we normally identify as "Particular Baptist" in the mid-seventeenth century are better termed "baptistic congregationalists."

---

[2] Matthew C. Bingham, *Orthodox Radicals: Baptist Identity in the English Revolution*, Oxford Studies in Historical Theology (Oxford: Oxford University Press, 2019).

This reconceptualizing of the identity of the early Baptists helps to illuminate how the logic of Congregationalism—a nonnational understanding of the church as composed of local congregations of visible saints—led some Congregationalists to the conclusion that baptism was to be reserved only for those who could attest to saving faith in Christ.[3] The Reformed arguments for infant baptism made the church *de jure* (not merely *de facto*, as all would have admitted, given the possibility of false professions of faith) a mixed community, made up of both the elect and some who may in time prove themselves not to be regenerate. If all of the infant children of believers are to become members of the church through baptism, then the church is, in principle, a mixed community (like Old Testament Israel) rather than a regenerate community (as the new covenant promise of Jer 31:34 seems to suggest). The Congregationalist rejection of this notion of a mixed church led some in their ranks to the Baptist position.

The story runs roughly as follows: The Reformers rejected the Roman Catholic *ex opere operato* ("by the work that is performed") understanding of baptism as a guarantee of regeneration. But by retaining the practice of infant baptism, this position necessitated an understanding of the church as a mixed community in principle. Some individuals may be Christians merely "externally and federally" but not "internally and savingly." Congregationalists eventually came to reject this mixed understanding of the church and the national church it underwrote. According to Congregationalists, the visible church is not to be identified with any national church but only with local congregations of visible, internal Christians. But Congregationalists retained the practice of infant baptism. This position proved to be unstable, as the "Half-Way Covenant"

[3] Here, we are retaining the standard usage of the label "Baptist."

controversy demonstrated (in this dispute, the question was whether or not infant-baptized non-church members could present their children for baptism). The Baptists, or baptistic congregationalists, simply carried the logic of Congregationalism to its necessary conclusion: if the church is made up of visible saints and if baptism is the entryway into the church, then baptism is only rightly administered to those who give credible evidence of conversion. It was not some kind of radical biblicism that led to this conclusion (though it was certainly grounded in the New Testament pattern), but the logic of Congregationalism and reformational theology that led to this position.

Bingham's argument is historically well documented, demonstrating from the primary sources that "Baptists" conceived of themselves as travelers along the "Congregational way." Many Congregationalists and Presbyterians also tended to locate Baptists within the Congregational movement. Bingham's work provides a helpful corrective to much of Baptist historiography, which has tended to import later concerns for denominational identity back onto the 1630s and 1640s. Bingham's theological acumen is also on display in his book. He grasps not only the historical record but the soteriological, ecclesiological, and sacramental issues at stake in these seventeenth-century debates. This book is highly recommended not only for Baptists wishing to better understand our historical and theological origins, but also for non-Baptists who are sometimes wont to misidentify all Baptists as "Anabaptists" and to miss the connections between the earliest Baptists and their fellow Reformed orthodox brethren.

A concern for a pure church is central to the Baptist vision. A commitment to a believers' church carries with it a corresponding commitment to the church's visible holiness. It is not that Christians are expected to lead a life of sinless perfection (though a total commitment to the way of Christ is always the goal). Baptists and many other reformational Christians have rejected the Wesleyan notion of "entire sanctification" or "Christian perfection," but Baptists have been concerned to fence the boundaries of the church both on the front end (by requiring a credible profession of faith for admittance to the baptismal waters, church membership, and Communion) and also on the backend (through the practice of church discipline). We now turn our attention to this "back door" of church discipline.

Church Discipline

Church discipline often has a bad reputation, sometimes for good reason. It conjures up images of exacting church leaders who expect perfection from the members and are ready to pounce at the slightest misstep. While church discipline has sometimes been applied in hasty and pastorally insensitive ways, it is not unbiblical in principle. Both Jesus and his apostles expected the church to correct its membership for errant beliefs and persistent unrepentance. The foundational text on church discipline comes from the Lord himself in Matt 18:15–20 (ESV):

> If your brother sins against you, go and tell him his fault, between you and him alone. If he listens to you, you have gained your brother. But if he does not listen, take one or two others along with you, that every charge may be established by the evidence of two or three witnesses. If he refuses to listen to them, tell it to the church. And if he refuses to listen even to the church, let him be to you as a Gentile and a tax collector. Truly, I say to you, whatever you bind on earth shall be bound in heaven, and whatever

> you loose on earth shall be loosed in heaven. Again I say to you, if two of you agree on earth about anything they ask, it will be done for them by my Father in heaven. For where two or three are gathered in my name, there am I among them.

Several noteworthy principles stand out in this passage. First, church discipline should follow a patient and orderly process. The order is clear: private correction, then with two or three others, and finally before the whole gathered assembly. Second, the final human authority under Christ's supreme lordship is not the church leaders or some ecclesiastical authority outside the local church but the whole congregation itself. Jesus does not say, "Tell it to the elders," but, "Tell it to the church (*ekklēsia*, the assembly)." Church officers ought to provide leadership and oversight, but it is the whole congregation that has been given the keys to the kingdom. Third, the goal of church discipline is restoration, not final renunciation. Church discipline is intended to be redemptive, not punitive. Even when church discipline ends in excommunication ("let him be to you as a Gentile and a tax collector," that is, an outsider to the church), the church should treat the disciplined member as Jesus treated Gentiles and tax collectors: as an object of love and evangelism. Fourth, the famous promise of the Lord's presence where "two or three are gathered" in his name is given precisely in this context of church discipline. The church is not infallible, but when it acts with due deliberation and according to biblical principles, it enjoys the very imprimatur of heaven itself through the Lord's gracious presence. In this high and holy task of preserving the purity of the church, local congregations rely on the authority and power of the Lord.

The apostles and their churches followed Jesus's teaching on the practice of church discipline. Paul instructs the Corinthian church to discipline a sexually immoral member who was living with his father's wife (1 Cor 5:1). The purpose was redemptive, not punitive: "hand that one over to Satan for the destruction of the flesh, so that his spirit may be saved in the day of the Lord" (1 Cor 5:5). The church is to maintain the purity of its membership, cleaning out the "old leaven" so that the congregation can remain a pure, unleavened bread in "sincerity and truth" (1 Cor 5:8). In 2 Cor 2:6, Paul urges the church to receive back a disciplined member who had repented. The "punishment by a majority is enough" for the person (indicating that some kind of congregational "vote" had taken place). This individual may have even been the same person who was to be excommunicated in 1 Corinthians; regardless of the specifics, the repentant believer is to be forgiven and consoled, not perpetually shunned by the church. Likewise, the apostle John urges his churches to discipline members for errant and divisive teaching (1 John 4:1–6).

While most Christian denominations have practiced some form of church discipline, up to and including excommunication (that is, exclusion from the Lord's Table), Baptists have been especially concerned with fencing the membership of the local church. Only believers are to be admitted to membership in the church (initiated through the waters of believers' baptism), and professing believers are expected to remain true to the doctrine and discipline of the Lord. Historically, Baptists have written entire church manuals on the order and practice of church discipline.[4]

Baptists have also recognized that church discipline is not merely a corrective measure. They have sometimes made a distinction between "formative" and "corrective" discipline. The latter takes place in instances of serious doctrinal error or of persistent

[4] See the rich collection of Baptist ecclesiological manuals in Mark Dever, ed., *Polity: Biblical Arguments on How to Conduct Church Life* (Washington, DC: Center for Church Reform, 2001).

unrepentance, but the former takes place through the ordinary ministry of the church: the preaching of the Word, the observation of the Lord's Supper and the necessary self-examination that it demands (1 Cor 11:27–34), and the encouragement and accountability that should characterize the church's shared life together. The Baptist use of church covenants underscores both the formative and the corrective natures of church discipline. The Baptist vision for the church emerges from a particular interpretation of the biblical covenants, with the Old Testament covenants revealing in a progressive and promissory way the covenant of grace that is only definitively revealed and established in the new covenant. Each local assembly is brought under the lordship of Christ as a covenanted congregation. Our individual and collective faith in Christ is formed in covenant relationship to God and issues forth in covenant responsibilities toward one another. As one historic formula for these Baptist church covenants puts it,

> We engage, therefore, by the aid of the Holy Spirit, to walk together in Christian love; to strive for the advancement of this church, in knowledge, holiness and comfort; to promote its prosperity and spirituality; to sustain its worship, ordinances, discipline, and doctrines; to contribute cheerfully and regularly to the support of the ministry, the expenses of the church, the relief of the poor, and the spread of the Gospel through all nations…We further engage to watch over one another in brotherly love; to remember one another in prayer; to aid one another in sickness and distress; to cultivate Christian sympathy in feeling and Christian courtesy in speech; to be slow to take offense, but always ready for reconciliation and

> mindful of the rules of our Savior, to secure it without delay.[5]

Baptist churches are covenanted communities of visible saints who commit together to walk in the discipline and order of the Lord Jesus Christ. This covenant commitment entails certain solemn obligations we owe to one another, including prayer, accountability, and support in our shared pilgrimage as we journey on to the Celestial City.

Conclusion: Growth in Holiness

What does holiness look like on the ground in Baptist spirituality? Many answers to that question share much in common with other Christian traditions. But three areas are especially prominent in Baptist spirituality. First is our obligation to make diligent use of the ordinary means of grace. Baptist confessions and catechisms, like those of other Protestant traditions, have emphasized the Lord's "ordinances" as the ordinary means by which we are savingly united to the benefits of Christ: the Word, prayer, and the sacraments of baptism and the Lord's Supper. So, Baptist spirituality begins at church. There is a priority placed upon the regular, embodied assembly of Christ's people on the Lord's Day. Those practices of corporate worship are vital to the believer's growth in holiness: hearing the Word read and preached, participating in the prayers and praises of God's people, and observing the two sacraments of the church.

Worship cascades from the corporate gathering to the practice of family worship and the exercises of private worship and prayer. The heads of households have a special obligation to foster holiness

[5] J. Newton Brown, *Baptist Church Manual* (Philadelphia: American Baptist Publication Society, 1853), 23–24.

among the members of the family by regular family prayer, Bible reading, and worship. Each individual Christian also has a duty to seek the Lord daily through spiritual disciplines: Bible reading and meditation, personal prayer, silence, solitude, fasting, and the generous giving of our time and resources.[6]

The goal of all of these practices of corporate, family, and private devotion is union with God in Christ by the Holy Spirit. Growth in holiness takes place as we remain in Christ, as branches connected to the life-giving sap of the true vine (John 15). Baptist spirituality, like all genuine Christian spirituality, is concerned with the Spirit-wrought formation of the believer into Christlikeness: to have the character of Christ formed in us (Gal 4:19), to be conformed to his image (Rom 8:29), and to be transformed into that same image by beholding the glory of the Lord (2 Cor 3:18; see also 1 Cor 15:49; Col 1:15; 3:10; 1 John 3:2). The beauty of Baptist spirituality is that it holds the personal and the communal dimensions of this process of growth in tension. We must exercise our own individual agency in our spiritual formation, but we do so in the context of the covenanted assembly of the church.

---

[6] One of the leaders of the twentieth-century revival of interest in the disciplines was philosophy professor Dallas Willard, who was also a Southern Baptist minister. See Dallas Willard, *Divine Conspiracy: Rediscovering Our Hidden Life in God* (New York: Harper, 1998) and Dallas Willard, *The Spirit of the Disciplines: Understanding How God Changes Lives* (New York: HarperOne, 1999). See also Donald S. Whitney, *Spiritual Disciplines for the Christian Life*, rev. ed. (Colorado Springs: NavPress, 2014).

CHAPTER 12

Mission

Introduction

The Great Commission uniquely encapsulates the main contours of the Baptist vision (Matt 28:18–20). The risen Lord Jesus Christ, who as the divine King already possesses all authority, has been granted all authority in heaven and on earth as the Davidic King through his incarnate obedience (see Rom 1:4). As the glorified God-man, he commissions his church to make disciples among all nations. Having given them this mission, he does not leave them to their own devices to determine the best methods for carrying it out. Instead, he has also instructed the church how they are to accomplish this global mission: by going into all the world, by baptizing new converts in the triune name, and by teaching them to observe all of his commandments. In the Greek text of this passage, there is only one finite verb, which is the central imperative of the Great Commission: make disciples, or learners, in the school of Jesus Christ. This central command is accompanied by three participial phrases, which may be interpreted as the means for carrying out the command, or else as three attending circumstances to the fundamental mission of making disciples: going, baptizing, and teaching. Baptists believe that this mission has been given to the whole church, not just its ordained officers or special envoys. Every believer and every local church is duty bound to spread the fame of Jesus Christ far and wide. In this final chapter, we will home in on this fundamental Baptist concern: a life of mission.

Mission and the Baptist Distinctives[1]

Properly speaking, mission is not a Baptist distinctive. All Christian denominations have felt the weight of the Great Commission and sought opportunities to evangelize the various peoples of the earth. We might think of the various ways the gospel spread throughout the Roman Empire and beyond in the early centuries of the church. We might also mention the mission of St. Patrick to the Celtic peoples of Ireland, or of St. Augustine of Canterbury to the Saxons in the sixth century, or other missionary activities throughout church history.

Mission is very close to the heart of the Baptist vision for the church and the Christian life. As we suggested in the section on Baptist distinctives, a commitment to the liberty of the individual conscience is fundamental to what it means to be a Baptist. The imaginative and influential Southern Baptist theologian E. Y. Mullins described this distinctive under the rubric, "soul competency."[2] While it is possible for this focus on individual freedom to be abused when it is untethered from biblical authority and congregational accountability, it nevertheless captures something central to the Baptist vision. No one can believe for you. There is no notion of "proxy faith" in the Baptist vision. No one is born into the kingdom

---

[1] Portions of this section first appeared in R. Lucas Stamps, "The Baptist Ideal: Religious Freedom in an Age of Moral Confusion," *The Center for Baptist Renewal*, September 19, 2023, https://www.centerforbaptistrenewal.com/blog/2023/9/19/the-baptist-ideal-religious-freedom-in-an-age-of-moral-confusion.

[2] E. Y. Mullins, *Axioms of the Christian Religion: A New Interpretation of the Baptist Faith* (Philadelphia: Griffith and Roland, 1908).

of God by virtue of birth, parentage, or national origin. We must be "born again" to enter into the new covenant people of God. This emphasis entails a corresponding commitment to religious liberty. Baptists envision a "free church in a free state" as the "Baptist ideal."[3] The state has jurisdiction over the so-called second table of the law of God: our obligations toward our fellow humans. It should provide safe passage for the dissemination of the gospel and should not seek to encroach upon the church's uniquely religious charge.

Baptist history includes voices arguing for a comprehensive form of religious liberty that was ahead of its time. For example, one of the earliest Baptists, Thomas Helwys, wrote that the king may not "be judge between God and man. Let them be heretics, Turks, Jews, or whatsoever, it appertains not to the earthly power to punish them in the least measure."[4] On the other hand, some Baptist luminaries argue for a more muscular Christian magistracy. For example, John Gill, arguably the most important eighteenth-century Baptist theologian, argued that a Christian king has a duty to enforce not only the second table of the law (laws governing love of neighbor) but also the first table of the law (laws governing love of God):

> Kings are the guardians of the laws of God and man; and Christian kings have a peculiar concern with the laws of the two tables, that they are observed, and the violaters of them punished; as sins against the first table, idolatry, worshipping of more gods than one, and of graven

[3] "XVII: Religious Liberty," *The Baptist Faith and Message* 2000, The Southern Baptist Convention, https://bfm.sbc.net/bfm2000/#xvii.

[4] Thomas Helwys, *A Short Declaration on the Mystery of Iniquity*, ed. Richard Groves (Macon, GA: Mercer University Press, 1998), 53.

> images, blaspheming the name of God, perjury, and false swearing, and profanation of the day of worship.[5]

Despite this diversity, the consistent accent in Baptist political theology has been placed upon religious liberty. Inviting the magistrate to prosecute matters of religion is a minority report in Baptist history. Baptist leaders often made the best of their political circumstances, but the consistent drumbeat was for freedom of religious expression and the separation of the civil and ecclesiastical powers. The Baptist confessional tradition represents this consensus Baptist view more accurately than any individual Baptist author. For example, the influential Second London Baptist Confession of Faith, which followed the establishmentarian Westminster Confession of Faith in most respects, tellingly omitted the mention of "piety" as a jurisdiction of the magistrate and entirely left out the paragraph outlining the magistrate's role as a "nursing father" who has charge to "protect the church of our common Lord."[6] Instead, what we find in the Baptist confession is an affirmation of the state's crucial but limited role of maintaining public justice and peace. The maintenance of evangelical piety and the business of the gospel are the exclusive jurisdiction of the church of the Lord Jesus Christ.

Whatever we make of the variegated Baptist tradition, the key concern for contemporary Baptists on questions of political theory should be Baptist biblical and theological logic, not simply Baptist history. The most relevant question is not, What were the historically contingent opinions of specific Baptists (often under duress)

---

[5] John Gill, *A Complete Body of Doctrinal and Practical Divinity*, 2 vols. (Grand Rapids: Baker, 1978), 2:746.

[6] For a tabular comparison of the two confessions on this article, see "A Tabular Comparison of the 1646 WCBF and the 1689 LCBF," accessed January 25, 2024, https://www.proginosko.com/docs/wcf_lbcf.html#WCF23.

in various political arrangements? but rather, What are the political entailments of Baptist biblical theology and ecclesiology? Baptists should be concerned with the ideal when it comes to political theology and the mission of the church.

The Baptist Faith and Message 2000, the confessional statement of the Southern Baptist Confession, answers this very question in its article on religious liberty:

> The gospel of Christ contemplates spiritual means alone for the pursuit of its ends. The state has no right to impose penalties for religious opinions of any kind . . . A free church in a free state is the Christian ideal, and this implies the right of free and unhindered access to God on the part of all men, and the right to form and propagate opinions in the sphere of religion without interference by the civil power.[7]

The Baptist vision is founded on the notion of "free and unhindered access to God on the part of all men." The Baptist commitment to a believers' church and the corollary commitment to believers-only baptism presuppose the dignity and freedom of the individual in matters of religion. The shift from the old covenant to the new covenant signals a reconstitution of the people of God, grounded not in parentage but in personal faith in Jesus Christ.[8] True saving faith cannot be coerced. Individuals are not born into the church in the same way they are born into the family or the state. They must be

---

[7] "XVII: Religious Liberty," *The Baptist Faith and Message 2000.*

[8] For a critique of the recent movements related to "Christian Nationalism" through the lens of Baptist theology, see Matthew Y. Emerson, "Is It Possible to Be a Baptist Christian Nationalist?" *9Marks Journal* (April 28, 2023), https://www.9marks.org/article/is-it-possible-to-be-a-baptist-christian-nationalist/.

born again for entrance into the new covenant people of God. If individuals are to be free to accept the claims of Christ, then they must be free to reject those claims as well. The wheat and the tares must grow together in the field of the world. The final sifting is not the prerogative of any earthly authority but the exclusive preserve of God himself through his holy angels at the end of the age (Matt 13:30). Interestingly, many of the early Baptists viewed evangelism as one of the primary motivations for religious liberty. For example, the erstwhile Baptist pioneer in America, Roger Williams, argued that non-Christian groups ("Jews, Turks, Antichristians, pagans") should not be persecuted for their beliefs precisely in order that they might be won over to repentance.[9]

Magisterial Protestants, those who believe that the civil magistrate partners with the church to maintain a Christian social order, agree that the government cannot coerce internal belief, but they also argue that a Christian state has the authority to restrict the external expression of contrary religious beliefs. A Christian state can, in principle, punish expressions of non-Christian belief (up to and including imprisonment and execution), though it may allow a degree of religious toleration as a matter of prudential judgment. All of this is inconsistent with the Baptist vision. Baptists are not content with a government that refuses to force feigned conversions but still presumes the authority to shut down peaceful religious dissent. There are limits to religious freedom: violence or other gross subversions of the social order are rightly proscribed. As the Baptist Faith and Message says in another context, "Freedom in any orderly

---

[9] Roger Williams, "The Bloody Tenent of Persecution," in *On Religious Liberty: Selections from the Works of Roger Williams*, ed. James Calvin Davis (Cambridge, MA: Belknap Harvard, 2008), 105.

relationship of human life is always limited and never absolute."[10] But provided these kinds of harm are not involved, the state is to give a wide berth to religious expression. The Baptist ideal is "a free church in a free state,"[11] which undergirds the church's evangelistic mission.

None of this suggests that Baptists are committed to a strictly secular society. Expressions of religious belief in the public square are not inconsistent with the Baptist vision. Baptists need not scrub "In God We Trust" from our currency or prohibit prayers at public events, and the Baptist vision certainly does not prevent the pursuit of legislation consistent with Christian ethical commitments. On the contrary, Baptists have been second to none in social action, which has been seen as an entailment of Christian mission. Consider, for example, the great Baptist missionary William Carey and his opposition to the Hindu practice of *sati*, the burning of widows on their husbands' funeral pyres.[12] Think of Andrew Fuller's opposition to the slave trade or Carl Henry's lifelong pursuit of Christian public engagement.[13] Or consider again the Baptist Faith and Message:

---

[10] "Article XVII: Religious Liberty," accessed June 18, 2024, *The Baptist Faith and Message* 2000, https://bfm.sbc.net/bfm2000/.

[11] "Article XVII: Religious Liberty," accessed June 18, 2024, *The Baptist Faith and Message* 2000, https://bfm.sbc.net/bfm2000/.

[12] See George, *Faithful Witness*, 149–52.

[13] In his 1803 sermon, "Christian Patriotism," Fuller states: "To prevent mistakes, however, it is proper to observe that the patriotism required of us is not that love of our country which clashes with universal benevolence, or which seeks its prosperity at the expense of the general happiness of mankind. Such was the patriotism of Greece and Rome; and such is that of all others where Christian principle is not allowed to direct it. Such, I am ashamed to say, is that with which some have advocated the cause of negro slavery. It is necessary, forsooth, to the wealth of this country! No; if my country cannot prosper but at the expense of justice, humanity, and the happiness of mankind, let it be unprosperous! But this is not the case. Righteousness will be found to exalt a nation, and so to be true wisdom." Baptist History Homepage, accessed January 25, 2024, http://baptisthistoryhomepage.com/

> In the spirit of Christ, Christians should oppose racism, every form of greed, selfishness, and vice, and all forms of sexual immorality, including adultery, homosexuality, and pornography. We should work to provide for the orphaned, the needy, the abused, the aged, the helpless, and the sick. We should speak on behalf of the unborn and contend for the sanctity of all human life from conception to natural death. Every Christian should seek to bring industry, government, and society as a whole under the sway of the principles of righteousness, truth, and brotherly love.[14]

Social action is an important part of Christian discipleship, especially the obligation to love our neighbors as ourselves. But social change is ultimately subordinate to and dependent upon the proclamation of the life-changing gospel of Jesus Christ. As the Baptist Faith and Message also says, "Means and methods used for the improvement of society and the establishment of righteousness among men can be truly and permanently helpful only when they are rooted in the regeneration of the individual by the saving grace of God in Jesus Christ."[15]

In sum, the Baptist ideal is a free church in a free state, and this political theory is grounded in a commitment to mission. It envisions a broad religious freedom within peaceful limits. It provides for Christians to be thoroughly engaged in the political process, bringing Christian commitments to bear on public policy. Even

---

fuller.sermon.partiotism.html; see also the influential 1947 manifesto, Henry, *The Uneasy Conscience of Modern Fundamentalism.*

[14] "Article XV: The Christian and the Social Order," accessed June 18, 2024, *The Baptist Faith and Message* 2000, https://bfm.sbc.net/bfm2000/.

[15] "Article XV: The Christian and the Social Order," accessed June 18, 2024, *The Baptist Faith and Message* 2000, https://bfm.sbc.net/bfm2000/.

more importantly, it recognizes the unique role of the church and its proclamation of the gospel as the only means for bringing about meaningful and lasting change for both individuals and society as a whole. As the church in the West faces unique challenges from an encroaching illiberalism on the Left and a sometimes fearful and confused reaction to it on the Right, this Baptist ideal is needed now more than ever.

International Missions

Anyone who grew up in a Baptist church knows the importance of international missions. In a Southern Baptist context, the tenor of every children's program was oriented in one way or another toward missions. Mission Friends, Royal Ambassadors, Girls in Action, and Vacation Bible School all underscored the necessity of world evangelization. Lottie Moon, the nineteenth-century missionary to China, was a household name, and the annual Christmas offering named in her honor was an essential part of our Christian discipleship. But none of this is unique to the Southern Baptist Convention. A stress on evangelism and mission is a consistent thread throughout the Baptist movement.

The modern missions movement was sparked by an association of Particular Baptist churches in early eighteenth-century London. William Carey, often considered the father of the modern missions movement, pioneered the cause through his courageous mission to India in 1793. His *Enquiry into the Obligations of Christians to Use Means for the Conversion of the Heathen* was a foundational text, as was *The Gospel Worthy of All Acceptation* penned by his Baptist compatriot, the theologian Andrew Fuller.[16] These men argued

[16] William Carey, *Enquiry into the Obligations of Christians to Use Means for the Conversion of the Heathen* (London: Carey Kingsgate, 1961); Andrew Fuller, *Gospel Worthy of All Acceptation*, 3rd ed. (Philadelphia: Charles Cist, 1805).

against the hyper-Calvinists of their day that divine predestination is not an impediment to global mission and the duty incumbent upon all to repent and believe in the gospel. The God who has ordained the end (the salvation of the elect) has also ordained the means of their salvation (the indiscriminate, global proclamation of the gospel). In a stirring account of his venture to India, Carey told Fuller and the other London Baptists, "I will go down into the pit, if you will hold the rope." Their efforts launched a renewed commitment on the part of Baptists and others to take the gospel to the ends of the earth.

In an American context, Adoniram Judson is often considered the father of modern missions in America. Commissioned as a Congregationalist missionary to India, Judson became convinced of Baptist distinctives while on the journey. His mission to Burma (Myanmar) became a catalyst to missionary zeal among Baptists in America.[17] His contemporary, Luther Rice, with the inspiration and support of Carey, helped to form the first mission-sending agency in America, which later became the Triennial Convention, the predecessor to the Southern Baptist Convention.

But even before Carey and Judson, another American Baptist minister had already been commissioned to international missions work. The freed slave George Liele, who was the first ordained African American Baptist minster in America (1775), was sent on mission to Jamaica in 1782. His ministry produced thousands of conversions among Jamaican slaves and became a hub for further missions in America and beyond. Despite persecution and

---

[17] For more on Judson's legacy, see Jason G. Duesing, ed., *Adoniram Judson: A Bicentennial Appreciation of the Pioneer American Missionary* (Nashville: B&H Academic, 2012).

imprisonment, Liele's mission to Jamaica was a remarkable success and eventually led to the eradication of slavery on the island.[18]

Other missionary giants could be mentioned, including Moon's influential ministry, Annie Armstrong and the formation of the Women's Missionary Union, and Bertha Smith's mission to China. Many of the heroes of Baptist missionary work are historically obscure but cherished by the families, churches, and associations who have sent them in Jesus's name to evangelize the nations. This rich legacy of Baptist missions continues to have a lasting effect on Baptist faith. Today, the International Mission Board of the Southern Baptist Convention has over 3,500 field personnel, making it the largest missionary force in the world. When other Baptist and baptistic denominations and organizations are included, the total number of missionaries reaches into the tens of thousands.

Domestic Missions

Baptists have been committed to evangelization not only to the uttermost parts of the world but also in our own Jerusalems, Judaeas, and Samarias (Acts 1:8). When the Southern Baptist Convention was formed in 1845, it established both a Foreign Mission Board (today's International Mission Board) and a Home Mission Board (today's North American Mission Board). The task of evangelism is both global and local. Some must be called out, trained, and commissioned to minister in cross-cultural contexts, but others remain relatively closer to home as church planters, evangelists, and directors of local mission. Annie Armstrong, like Lottie Moon, is a household name among Southern Baptists, through the annual Easter offering collected in her honor to support home missions.

---

[18] Lesley Hildreth, "Missionaries You Should Know: George Liele," *International Mission Board*, June 26, 2018, https://www.imb.org/2018/06/26/missionaries-you-should-know-george-liele/.

Baptists have insisted upon personal evangelism as a universal Christian obligation. All Christians have been tasked with the Great Commission. Baptist churches have regularly practiced door-to-door evangelism and more fundamentally have urged all members to engage their family members, friends, and coworkers with the claims of Jesus Christ. Every Christian has a duty to "give a defense to anyone who asks you for a reason for the hope that is in you" (1 Pet 3:15). Baptist churches have also been active in planting new local assemblies of Christ followers. While some Baptist churches have, sadly, been formed as a result of church splits, many others were established as missions of existing churches.

Baptists have not always been known for their theologians, though there have been many skilled theologians in Baptist history. Baptists have been more marked by their missionaries, evangelists, and social reformers. Two of the most influential religious figures of the twentieth century were Baptists: the evangelist Billy Graham and the civil rights advocate Martin Luther King Jr. In their domestic missionary activity, Baptists have also been keen to start colleges, seminaries, hospitals, and various charitable organizations. Baptist mission is concerned with both gospel proclamation and social action, both the dissemination of sound doctrine and the practice of biblical charity.

Conclusion: The Goal of Missions

The final goal of Baptist missions is the worship of the triune God. While mission has been close to the heart of the Baptist vision, it gives way to a more ultimate concern. As Baptist preacher and author John Piper, has put it,

> Missions is not the ultimate goal of the church. Worship is. Missions exists because worship doesn't. Worship is ultimate, not missions, because God is ultimate, not man. When this age is over and the countless millions of the redeemed fall on their faces before the throne of God, missions will be no more. It is a temporary necessity. But worship abides forever.[19]

The goal of Baptist spirituality is not an endless quest for more converts. It is inviting those converts to follow the way of Jesus so that they can worship the one true God in spirit and in truth (John 4:23–24). By God's grace, Baptists seek to be like Evangelist, the character in John Bunyan's allegory *The Pilgrim's Progress*, who puts the protagonist, Christian, on the sure path to the Celestial City. The Baptist vision sets its gaze supremely on that heavenly city and invites every man, woman, boy, and girl to join us on this blessed pilgrimage. If the Baptist vision is to retain its spiritual vitality in the twenty-first century and beyond, it must keep both the penultimate goal of mission and the ultimate goal of true worship constantly in view.

---

[19] John Piper, *Let the Nations Be Glad: The Supremacy of God in Missions*, 3rd ed (Grand Rapids: Baker Academic, 2010), 35.

Conclusion: Toward the Baptist Future

In this book, we have attempted to explain and to celebrate the core commitments of the Baptist vision. The Baptist movement is grounded in a fundamental commitment to the lordship of Jesus Christ, as he is revealed in Holy Scripture and as he has been confessed and worshipped in historic Christian orthodoxy. Furthermore, the Baptist vision is committed to the soteriological principles of the Reformation, to the distinctive spirituality of evangelicalism, and to a particular way of reading the unfolding biblical drama. These commitments issue forth in a particular way of being the church, one committed to liberty of conscience, believers' baptism, covenantal Communion, congregational government, and religious liberty. Finally, this Baptist vision is lived out in the context of worship, holiness, and mission.

We believe that the Baptist vision offers a biblically, theologically, and spiritually compelling way of being a Christian. There are other ways, to be sure, and Baptists have much to receive and benefit from in the great treasury of traditions that constitute the one, holy, catholic, apostolic church. Baptists have much to contribute as well. As we conclude, we wish to offer several humble suggestions that Baptists might follow to ensure that our vision continues to provide the faithful with a clear-eyed path to the Celestial City, despite all the obstacles and temptations we face in the twenty-first century.

First, Baptists have a fundamental obligation to continue teaching our people the biblical story. Baptists are a people of the book. We hold the Scriptures to be the supreme source and standard for all faith and practice, but biblical illiteracy can subvert this vision. Pastors, parents, Sunday School teachers, and all believers have a duty to "read, hear, and understand the holy scriptures" and to pass this knowledge on to others.[1] Our people need to know the stories, and "the Story," of the Bible. They must learn of the creation, fall, patriarchs, exodus, judges, kings, psalmists, sages, prophets, apostles, and apocalypse. But they also must be taught the dramatic arc that is communicated through these stories, which is centered on the person and work of Jesus Christ, the "key" to unlocking all the treasures of divine knowledge (Luke 11:52).

Second, Baptists should prioritize an "ordinary means of grace" ministry. The early Baptists believed that the ordinary way that sinners receive the benefits of Christ's redemptive work are his "ordinances," that is, the practices he put in order so that we might be united to him: the preaching of the Word, the celebration of baptism and of the Lord's Supper, and prayer.[2] Baptists may enact many other ministries and programs for the edification of the church and the spread of the gospel, but these ordinances are nonnegotiable. Our spiritual formation must be ordered to these central acts of corporate worship.

Third, Baptists need to do a better job than we sometimes have of positioning the Baptist movement within the historic Christian church. At its best, the Baptist vision is not sectarian. The early Baptists did not seek to found a new religion or to suggest that

---

[1] "The Baptist Catechism, Question 5," in *The Baptist Confession and the Baptist Catechism* (Birmingham: Solid Ground, 2010).

[2] "The Baptist Catechism, Question 93," in *The Baptist Confession and the Baptist Catechism.*

Christians must begin from scratch in each new generation. In their confessional symbols, they intentionally and deliberately sought to restate the creedal beliefs that lie at the foundation of the Christian religion. So, contemporary Baptists have nothing to fear from a deep study of church history. Retrieval for the sake of renewal should be our watchword. We can retain our Baptist distinctives and still learn a great deal from the church fathers, the ancient creeds and councils, the medieval scholastics and mystics, the Reformers and their heirs, and faithful expositors of Scripture both near and far. The Baptist vision is not a counterinsurgency; it is a renewal movement from within the universal church.

Fourth, Baptists should remain courageously committed to sound doctrine and biblically based social action. The best of our tradition has kept these things together. In the face of false doctrine, Baptists should remain committed to trinitarian, Christological, anthropological, and soteriological orthodoxy. In the face of moral confusion, Baptists must remain steadfast in our commitments to the dignity of all human life (from conception to natural death), to liberty of conscience, to the goodness of biblically defined gender and sexuality, to racial justice, and to the duties of mercy shown to the poor, the oppressed, the abused, and the outcast. These convictions are only as good as our commitment to personal doctrinal fidelity and to a life of visible holiness, as a people bearing witness to the coming kingdom.

Finally, Baptists should continue to do what Baptists have historically done best: to proclaim the life-giving message of Jesus Christ to the ends of the earth. The mission is urgent. Both time and eternity hang in the balance. Baptists, along with all true believers, have the only message that can save sinners from their harrowing plight: from "all miseries in this life," from "death itself," and from "the pains of hell for ever."[3] Only Jesus can save, and only the church has been uniquely commissioned by Jesus to be ambassadors of his gospel. Thus, we should redouble our efforts to call out, train, and commission envoys of the gospel to every people group on earth. We should all recommit ourselves to bear witness to the gospel in our families, neighborhoods, and workplaces. If the Baptist vision is to remain a vibrant part of the church in the twenty-first century and beyond, it must focus its lenses unswervingly on the only Word that can redeem and reconcile sinners to God: "Jesus Christ and him crucified" (1 Cor 2:2). God grant us grace to remain faithful to our Lord's Commission. To that end, we conclude with the Apostle Paul's closing doxology in his letter to the Romans:

> Now to him who is able to strengthen you according to my gospel and the preaching of Jesus Christ, according to the revelation of the mystery that was kept secret for long ages but has now been disclosed and through the prophetic writings has been made known to all nations, according to the command of the eternal God, to bring about the obedience of faith—to the only wise God be glory forevermore through Jesus Christ! Amen.
> (Rom 16:25–27 ESV)

[3] "The Baptist Catechism, Question 22," in *The Baptist Confession and the Baptist Catechism.*

Name and Subject Index

Scripture Index